Ickerbrow Trig

Michael Haslam

Ickerbrow Trig

Shearsman Books

First published in the United Kingdom in 2020 by
Shearsman Books Ltd
PO Box 4239
Swindon
SN3 9FN

Shearsman Books Ltd Registered Office
30–31 St. James Place, Mangotsfield, Bristol BS16 9JB
(this address not for correspondence)

www.shearsman.com

ISBN 978-1-84861-697-4

ACKNOWLEDGEMENTS

'The Quiet Works' was published as a pamphlet by Oystercatcher Press in
2009; 'Old Lad' appeared in *The Cambridge Literary Review* (No. 5, 2011)
and also in *The Best British Poetry 2012* (Salt Publications); 'What I Do Mean'
appeared in *Snow lit rev* No. 1, 2013; the final version of 'Party Spirits' was
rewritten for R.F. Langley in London, June 2011; the Postscript was written
on hearing of Roger's death in 2011, and included by Jeremy Noel-Tod in his
introduction to Langley's *Complete Poems* (Carcanet 2015); 'A Round Word:
World' appeared in *Shearsman* (97 & 98, Winter 2013/2014), guest-edited
by Kelvin Corcoran; 'Scaplings' was published on my 70th birthday 2017 by
Calder Valley Poetry; '16/2/47' was published in *The World Speaking Back to
Denise Riley* (Boiler House Press 2018).

Contents

On Ickerbrow Trig

Ickerbrow Trig, the book, is simply a collection of poems written since *A Cure for Woodness*. As the book title it's simply the remnant of a bonnet-bee and an exhausted pun. As a topographical feature it exists, un-named as such on any map.

I came to live at Foster Clough, on the Heights Road (misnamed 'Height Road' by the Ordnance Survey) along the Midgley moor-edge, in 1970. One early guide to the moor above was Jack Ingham, a gardener and poacher, retired. Jack reckoned that he knew the moor as well as anyone, including his one-time neighbour Stansfield Bolton the gamekeeper, when they'd both lived on the terrace of Foster Clough in the 1930s. Another of my guides was the Ordnance Survey. They didn't always agree on the names of features.

Jack took me up to Walton Edge (not on the map), a much-quarried edge of sandstone and, after a diversion over Crow Hill (one of three Crow Hills in the vicinity) we viewed Folly Field, where, Jack said, there used to be held Whitsun Fairs, with stalls and a brass band. We wandered hither and thither by the Limers Gate, Robin Hood's Penny Stone, Miller's Grave, and the trig point on Cock Hill (one of three Cock Hills on this same moor). Then we took in the view across the slack of Dimmin Dale, to another trig-point on the skyline. That, said Jack, is Ickerbrow, and then, pointing to the edge of a shelf below it, that is Netherbrow.

Clearly, Ickerbrow was higher brow, and Netherbrow was lower brow. But when I turned to my other guide, the O.S., I found different names than these. There was High Brown Knoll, and High Brown Knoll Edge, with Low Brown Knoll below. Now Ickerbrow has a sort of knoll, a bedrock outcrop, less prominent though than the trig point, or a standing stone nearby. (Our standing stones are largely historical boundary stones, and lack prehistorical resonance.) Netherbrow has no visible knoll, though it does have an edge, a brow. And I got this bee in my bonnet, that the O.S. mistake here was (though the moorland is often brownish) to read *brown* for *brow* when sounded before *knoll*. And it seems I was wrong. There's a rather rough Christopher Saxton map of 1594, among his maps of

Yorkshire Estates that depicts *High Browne Knowl* and *Low Browne Knowl*. I suppose this could have been a higher brow mistranslation of vernacular knowledge. *Ickerbow* and *Netherbrow* could have pre-existed Saxton and been held locally as a lowerbrow knowledge for generations by such as didn't need the Ordnance Survey to know where they were. I prefer them for euphony and accuracy. The O.S. 1841 map drops the *e* off *Brown* but holds to *Knowl*. By 1852 *Knowl* has become *Knoll*. My unlikely poetical ambition would be to re-instate *Ickerbrow*. It's a well-known spot, under its O.S. name, for fellrunners. And, does it matter? Why am I telling you this? There are readers who may find the prose of an Introduction easier to read than the poetry. It's these readers I'm trying to lead, like Willy Wisp, into the quags of Dimmindale Slack, under Netherbrow Edge.

I've already betrayed my bad and exhausted pun. I had thought to call this book *High Brow Knoll Edge Poems*, in some ironical reference to my supposed affiliation to 'Cambridge Poetry'. From that knoll edge we look down on our surroundings. But I wearied of the pun. Why not just *Ickerbrow Knoll*? Or then, *Ickerbrow Trig*, for trig points, obsolete, redundant, are (in conception, though the concrete ones date from the 1930s) coeval with the Industrial Revolution, and quite as venerable as disappearing words, some still in use, as *snicket, goit, bent, rough, sike* and *clough*, and other bits of landscape stuff that might delight a rhyming poet.

There'll be no further mention of Ickerbrow Trig in this book. It's just a title and a reference point at 443 metres (1453 feet, on an older map). I'll leave it on the skyline there, before I change my mind again. And no longer argue but credit the Ordnance Survey with plumping that whitewashed concrete lump by the knoll on the higher brow.

On the use of the lower case for named features

I might mention again, as I have done before, why it is that I don't choose to capitalise place names, some real, some typical, some invented. This practice I began around the turn of the millennium. Most of our place-manes are plain description, though often in an obsolescent vocabulary. I have not tried to distinguish these from such as are, very probably, personal names. I might like to think that Foster was Forester Clough, but it was more probably named for a Mr Foster. And, was there a Mr Walton who first delved into the brow of a flagstone edge, above the heights road below?

I may be about to abandon this practice, and in 2018 I restored upper-case place-names in the case of *16/2/47* (see below) and in the final sequence, *The Wooden Glade*. But the interest remains, and the reader is encouraged to glimpse holiness in Halliwell, oats in Havercroft, and bloomeries in Smithills. These places are to the North and West of Bolton-le-Moors in Lancashire (see below).

On *16/2/47*

This is a sequence of numbers I have been called on, regularly, to write or to recite. I have been known to take an unwonted pride in having been born at possibly the hardest point of the hardest winter of the 20th Century. My mother told me of the circumstances of my birth, but I thought for a while that I had some memory of the trauma since, in the 1970s a girlfriend drew me into the miasmic world of 'therapy', and a group-session involving 'rebirthing'. It went horribly wrong: there was no-one to beat me into life, and I passed a couple of days as one of the living dead.

The poem was first made for a photographer, Jemimah Kuhfeld, for a book of photographs of poets, with poems. I don't think the book ever appeared. Later the poem was part of an exhibition at Hebden Bridge Railway Station, organised by Sarah Corbett. It was up there as a poster for a month or so.

The poet Denise Riley's birthday is 16/2/48, and *16/2/47* was published in *The World Speaking Back to Denise Riley* (Boiler House Press 2018).

On *Party Spirits (third version)*

This is the third regarbling of *Party Spirits*. The first version was made for *Sneak's Noise*, a tribute to the poet R.F. Langley on his

60ᵗʰ birthday, published by Peter Riley and Nigel Wheale, and read at a party in Shropshire in 1998. A second version was in my *A Sinner Saved By Grace* (Arc 2005). The final version was rewritten for a memorial for R.F. Langley in London, June 2011. The *Postscript* was written (in tears!) on hearing of Roger's death (in 2011), and included by Jeremy Noel-Tod in his introduction to RFL's *Complete Poems* (Carcanet 2015).

What prompted the poem was this. Though I could defend myself against an accusation, in some ecclesiastical court, that I *believed in the fairies*, I do see supernaturals, fairies, ghosts, gods, as prime elements of the human imagination. And it's nobody's business if I write poetry in conversation with a familiar spirit. I called it 'the tail-end of spirit and two thirds of wit'. I imagined a competition to guess the name of the spirit. Roger Langley called it *Jack*, and I knew it was that. Jack exists, a common spirit, beyond belief. Of course, in folklore he could be Tom-Tit-Tot. And maybe our local moorland spur, Tom Tittiman, is named for some relation of his. I'd say I've had the local boggart as my familiar spirit, but someone might suppose I really mean it. It's just Imagination, honestly. I believe in the imagination; I don't believe in belief. Other than *Jenny Greenteeth* I can't see any specific local references in *Party Spirits*.

On *The Quiet Works*

The Quiet Works was published by Peter Hughes as an Oystercatcher pamphlet in 2009. It was written after the contents of *A Cure for Woodness* (Arc 2010). Pamphlet production is generally speedier than book production.

There are poets who could be, and have been, accused of being 'Nature Worshippers', particularly when it comes to the matter of water. I imagine the scientifico-ecclesiastical court accusing me of just such an heresy. In my defence, I affirm my orthodox materialism, and tell how firmly I resist a strong feeling and the temptations of my familiar imp. I do not worship anything at all. Water is matter of physics and chemistry. My attraction to it is merely biological, and historical, industrio-historical, literary and geological.

I once had a book of local poetry from the early 20th Century. The poets were keen on celebrating our 'crystal' streams. Liars! It was not only that, back then, bleaching and dyeing, and other effluents of textile industry would sully the Calder river-system, but that, higher up, the waters would generally be brownish, algal, peaty, if not also ferrous and coaly. If you wanted crystal streams you should try some other geology. And ruins of early water-powered mills, as well as reservoirs and sewage works are part of my love object. My first vision of my adopted valley (on a school trip from Bolton to York, by train, around 1960) was of a series of what we called 'sewage farms'. The sewage farms and sufferings of people and water belong to a beloved textile and textual history, shared across the Pennines. Now the air and water are cleaner, there are more trees than there have been for two hundred years, and our apparent wealth is a matter of incomprehensible economic magic.

I imagine my poetry is driven, irresponsibly, by my irresponsible imp, and my job is to try, sometimes vainly, to correct it, politically, socially, scientifically. I do try, but often fail, to obfuscate the imp's attempts to sexualise our unremarkable landscape of bald moorland hills and irriguous wooded cloughs. I try to cover up their sexual parts with botany and zoology, and the laughter of the imp is that I seem to fail. We do agree, however, on the fact of a libidinal collapse that has come with age. But where I'd think to express a sad sense of loss, the imp finds my predicament extraordinarily, or ordinarily, funny, and is happy to see me appear as a dirty old man.

The meanings of place-names can be disputed, even by experts, and often elude standard dictionaries. These, in *The Quiet Works,* are my versions as I understand them. A *slack* is a dip in a ridge; a *hope* a valley; a *worth* a farm; a *mere* a lake; a *rake* a track traversing a hillside. A *delf* (also spelled *delph*) is a quarry. I prefer *delf* as closer to the verb *to delve*. A *sike* is a small stream, like the more northerly *beck* and *burn*. A *clough* is a cleft, here generally wooded with a brook within. I lifted a *dub* from *Gurnal Dubs* in Westmorland. A *goit* is a man-made channel. A *ginnel* is a snicket. A *shaw* is a wood. A *snicket* is a ginnel. *Troughing* is guttering. A *naze* is a nose of the moor. *Sally* is a goat-willow. A *holme* is a water-meadow. Oh, and a *shippon*'s a cow-house. Anyone who disagrees with any of these definitions can argue with me in the pub.

On *Three Discontinual Songs*
and *Three More Discontinual Songs*

These six pages, or some of them, were, in a sense 'published' somewhere. I was invited to contribute to a magazine, and I sent these, or some of them. I somehow thought there'd be a paper magazine. It was an 'online' journal. I seem to remember glancing at the result on my computer soon after. Later I spent several minutes trying to find these pages again, but I failed. I had only computerised because typewriters were becoming obsolete. I found the internet could be a useful reference library, and I use email and email attachments, but if there's something to be read I have to suffer discomfort or print it out.

Discontinual Songs was meant to echo *Continual Song*. After about 15 years of writing poetry, around the time Margaret Thatcher became Prime Minister, I decided I was on the wrong track, and had to start again with *Continual Song* (Open Township 1986; republished in *A Whole Bauble,* Carcanet 1995, and again in *Mid Life,* Shearsman 2007). An idea of *Continual Song* was that it could be read front to back or back to front or from the middle outwards or from the outside in. Each page was meant to be a discrete entity. But there was a fault. There were a few pages that were ill-disguised sequences, running merely front to back. I hoped no-one would notice. Perhaps they didn't, and haven't.

I computerised in the early 21st Century. A few years later, thanks to Peter Manson, I acquired a website which I called Continualesong: as if everything I did were part of one continual song. But in the early decades of the new century, believing that with the libidinal collapse I would cease making poems, I called what I was doing *discontinual songs.* And its first fruits were sent to this, lost to me, online site.

Any notes? The *laverock* is a lark; *birken* is birchen; *hollins* are hollies. An *ousel's* a blackbird; a *mistal,* or *mistall,* like a *shippon* is a form of cow-house; a *midden's* a dungheap.

On *Old Lad*

So I was writing my *discontinual songs,* when I was invited, by Boris Jardine, to contribute to a real paper magazine, *The Cambridge Literary*

Review (No.5 2011). I submitted what were, probably, Nos. *vii, viii, ix, & x,* which were accepted. But were my *discontinuals* meant to be discrete pages, or did these four compose a unidirectional sequence? I judged it was a matter of the latter and proposed calling the four pages *Old Lad.* This was accepted. There's still a flaw: there's an abortive personification of *drizzle,* a quasi-Elizabethan melancholiac, become conflated with the Old Lad, a fictional dying local farmer. But maybe I shall never be famous enough to have my flaws dissected. *Old Lad* was picked up and included in the Salt publication *The Best British Poetry 2012.*

A *croft* is a farm, and a *fold* encloses its yard. *Footings* are foundations. A *laithe* is a barn. A *carr* is a marsh. And *mollyblobs* are marsh marigolds.

On *What I Do Mean*

So henceforth I would revert to my post-*Continual Song* mode of writing sequences, with at least the illusion of having old Aristotle's beginnings, middles, and ends.

And the next invitation came from the fine poet Anthony Barnett, to contribute to his new magazine, *Snow. What I Do Mean* appeared in *Snow No. 1,* 2013. Here the setting reverts to the Lancashire of my childhood, in which *Jenny Greenteeth* and *Nelly Long-arms,* both water-spirits, used often to lure me into their domain. In Lancashire *water* can rhyme with *matter.*

On its second page there's mention of *Back Progress Street.* This signifies an image of transitory reality that predates my attraction to poetry. It might have been, say, 1959. I used to travel home from my posh school, Bolton School, to Astley Bridge by walking through Queen's Park and catching one of five Bolton Corporation buses travelling north along the Blackburn Road. One afternoon the bus was stopped just up from where the Blackburn Road is crossed by Halliwell Road and Waterloo Street. Glancing out of the bus window I was struck by an abject view of slum dereliction, bearing the street-name *Back Progress Street.* Pure poetry! Within a year or two these dwellings had been demolished. I have not been back there for many years, but I've taken a look at the site by means of Google Earth. Many of the old mills have gone and much of the housing has been replaced. It all looks very clean. And up Blackburn Road one can see moorland. That never used to happen except during the June or September Holidays. There was so much smoke. And where was Progress Street there's now a clean and impressive mosque. Is that progress? There's emotion in my sense of the story of the Pennine textile industry, but lament or a sense of Good Riddance is beside the point. History is a pool of squalor into which I like to dip.

One branch of the *Astley Brook* rises near *Haslam's Farm* on *Smithills Moor,* another by *Holden's Farm* close to *The Two Lads* on *Rivington Moor,* and together they flow beneath *Astley Bridge* to meet the *Eagley Brook* at *Waters' Meetings,* or, as the O.S. will have it, *Meeting of the Waters.* Then the two brooks become the *River Tonge* which may be named for the tongue of land between it and the *Bradshaw Brook.*

By the fourth page we seem to have moved up the *Rochdale Canal* towards the promised land of *The West Riding of Yorkshire.* The *Watergrove Reservoir* and *Hades Hill* are up the *Ash Brook,* behind *Smallbridge,* between *Littleborough* and *Rochdale.* The disconsolate spooks are an insistent image of my imp, who is himself not at all disconsolate. I don't know what they, or he, or it, or the image means. Perhaps he does.

On *A Round Word: World*

Some Shakespearian scholars have used what might be contemporary reference to such things as the weather to date the plays. So, for instance, Titania's speech about bad summer weather *(A Midsummer Night's Dream AII; Sc1)* is taken as evidence for the play's composition soon after the bad summer of 1594, when the nine-men's morris was filled up with mud. *A Round Word: World* was written, I seem to recall, shortly before its publication in the magazine *Shearsman* (97&98, Winter 2013/2014) an edition guest-edited by Kelvin Corcoran. But I can detect the influence in the poem of a pub-visit to the Kilnsey Show in 2004. What I now remember of this event is now mainly my eavesdropping on a couple of Dales farmers, and barely understanding a word — *yowes,* yes, and App'ick (for Appletreewick), but no more than that. I count myself a Northerner but a couple of other times, half-a-century ago, I found myself baffled by my incomprehension of Northern speech. Once it was a truck-driver from Sheffield I failed to understand. More embarrassingly, once it was the talk in a Miners' Club at Boothstown, just off the East Lancs Road, only about five miles from my home. In those days there were still coalmines in Lancashire. I'd have had more clue as to what they were on about if they'd spoken French. I've been accused of being some sort of left-winger, but in my admiration for incomprehensible dialects of England, or my holding to the pre-1974 Counties of England, and my nostalgia for the remnants of Municipal Socialism, I am rather deeply conservative,

Another influence I can detect is that of the Waite pack of Tarot cards, and the Major Trump, The World. It's forty years since I messed with those cards, but Patricia Colman Smith's images have stuck. The naked World! It's an awkward time these days when heterosexual admiration may be accused of misogyny.

On *Scaplings, Star Jelly, and a Seeming Sense of Soul*

Living a hermit-like existence on the moor-edge, I had failed to notice the arrival in the Upper Calder Valley of a new generation of poets, including award-winners, University Creative Writing teachers, and allsorts. Some years ago Peter Riley settled in the valley and decided to investigate. His results were a revelation to me. One result was of his publishing *Pennine Tales* with Bob Horne's Calder Valley Poetry. Now, I reckon I've been writing, almost exclusively, Calder Valley poetry since around 1980, so I approached Bob. The result was, for short, *Scaplings,* published on my 70th birthday 2017. I wanted it to be a sort of climax, a tour de force – a phrase that, though school tried to teach me French, first really impressed me back in those days in a sleeve note by Orrin Keepnews to a Riverside record of Jelly Roll Morton's Library of Congress recordings, referring specifically to *Creepy Feeling.*

Doug Robbins, stonemason, was, while broad Yorkshire, slow, precise and deliberate in his use of language, and I'm sure that *scaplings* was the word he used. A friend suggested that it could have been *scalpings* – the shavings of newly cast steel that can be recycled (unlike *swarf* which is bound for the bin). No. But it made me think I could have made something, somewhere, of a cluster: shape, scape, scope, shave, scalp, sculpt, scrape &c., the point being not to elevate some quasi-mystical etymological original, but that clusters form on largely aesthetic grounds. If, as the French Theorists, my life's great nuisances have it "the linguistic sign is arbitrary" then, as with a dictator's arbitrary decisions, *arbitrary* must mean *chosen,* though without due process. We can perhaps exempt bureaucrats, lawyers, and scientists, but by choice is how poets, comedians, and common folk use language.

As a *tour de force, Scaplings* draws on my whole life, regardless of chronology. For paid labour there's reference to building work in the 1970s, engineering at the turn of the Century, and in textile recycling shortly thereafter. Much of my adult life has been to do with recycling: of buildings, of timber, of textiles, of vocabulary.

Vocabulary? Some words could have borne capitals for, though for the most part etymologically decipherable, they are best seen as specific. I'm thinking of the old townships that ring the upper valley: from the East, anticlockwise: Midgley, Wadsworth, Heptonstall, Stansfield, Todmorden-with-Walsden, Langfield, Erringden, and Sowerby. But a sike that trickles across a bank, comes to a brink, falls into a clough, and at some clough hole drops into a lumb before joining the river at some mytholm, could be any of several waters, brooks, or becks, but would signify this valley, the love-object of the work.

Scroggy is actually Scots but describes a *shroggs,* a scrubby area of woodland, happen with *ellers, ollers, birks, withens,* and *wicken.* If you rid a shroggs of its growth you may have a *royd,* cognate with *road* and *ride.* And a *lad law* is a boundary stone. I could go on but I'm stumped as a stubbings by not knowing meanings for *turley* (a proper name?) or *gorple* (surely some landscape term). So I retire to laik with delfstone and scaplings in our local gritstone delf.

The Wooden Glade

I am not a great dreamer of actual dreams. At one time I'd wake with no more than meaningless phrases such as *you could have socked me with a spider.* Another was simply *the wooden glade.* This latter phrase I came to insert in poems, published or aborted. The phrase came free of associations, so it was merely recondite, but perhaps no more so than references I'd made to *a long green hallway,* or the death of King George VI. Some things I might claim to discover, but, beyond that, I should have to invent. My invention was thus: the long green hallway and the death of the King belong, with other things, in the wooden glade. So what are some of these other things in the glade? An odd outlier for a wooden glade might be a toy sword. I had an answer for that. The wooden glade could be a *wooded* glade, but the touch of artifice might suggest the glades of Shakespearean pastoral. There is mental *woodness* in the wooden glade. Or the glade could be a disused delf (a mile up out of Mytholmroyd) that has been re-used as a place to laik or grow potatoes in. And then what's to be found in this Arden forest? There's the moments of infantile self-consciousness, and the self-conscious moments when sliding into some sexual congress, or in the discovery of self-abuse. And last, but largest, there's an irreducible core of poetry resistant to, and defiant of, psychology, philosophy, religion, or politics, and there's all my continual song from beginning to end.

Last Words

In the first and last poems of *Ickerbrow Trig, 16/2/47* and *The Wooden Glade,* I resile from my decades-long practice of writing place-names in the lower case. My purpose in the practice has been essentially didactic: to draw attention to the fact that the poetic element in a place-name is its topographical exactitude. So, for instance, my paths down to Mytholmroyd (a clearing at the waters' meetings) go by Stoney Lane, which is stony, and Dark Lane, which is sunken and dark. Halliwell and Blackburn mean what they are. I could invent places and, happen, later find their coincident actualities.

Urban street-names, however, are often almost meaningless cultural frivolities (Newnham Street, for instance). So much for that. What else is there to say, apart from that there's an invented place-name in the upper-case in *The Wooden Glade*? Ought else? I hold to my old contention that in the case of Ickerbrow, or High Brown Knoll, it is the consonant of knoll that has turned the brow brown. And, last, how odd it has been to have been anyone at all.

Part One

From Birth to the Old Age Pension

16/2/1947—16/2/2012

16/2/47

Snow fell from heaven while Aneurin Bevan
thought to spawn the NHS. Mother had drunk
her Guinness bottles on prescription nonetheless.
    Snow fell cold and soft on fold and croft.
Snow fell on Halliwell. Snow drifted into windrow
and an even swell. Snow overwhelmed the mill,
the mine, the railwayline. The world was frozen
in a shell of economic standstill. Snow blown over
Smithills Moor and Winter Hill had heaped against
the hospital, up to the window-sill.
    Such beauty thrills that still receptacle,
the unborn soul, a perfect hole. Snow fills
(rare phrase this for Northern England) Shaly Dingle:
Curl and cornice, turquoise light in ice crevasse.
Each being singularly single and subject
to chimes and tingle, such epiphanies as this'll
once or twice happen have come to pass.
    Snowfall bridges ridge and gable. Snow drifts up
by Hollin Wood. Sub-zero air, a few lights twinkle, but
the power cuts at night. The gate-stoup wind-side ice
withstood. Snow fell on Havercroft and Heaton: White.
    Blue, limply furled, cord-strangled, almost lifeless
as the nurses thump and batter, I was beaten
into breath: At last, some minutes old, I do protest
about my own ejection into this cold world. I'm told
it was a matter, simply, of my life or death.

Party Spirits *(third version)*

This game we call it *Guess the Name*
of what it is, that animated little gist
of something tickling in the brain; that impish
whatnot hidden in the verbiage disporting stuff---
Could it be *Spirit*? *Spirit!* I'd be just about
to shout out loud but stumble into doubt,
for it proliferates, with *Spurt* and *Sprite*,
or *Spurge* if verbiage means vegetation,
think of wrinkled wee green men.
Or look out *Spit* sits out upon my own tongues tip---
I could be wrong, and swallow my suggestion back.
Then *Roger Langley* calmly calls it *Jack*.
And we knew it was that.

The game's been won, and time winds down.
Hick fidgets. *Hob* looks to the clock,
while *Ken* and *Tom* begin discussing getting back.
Nan takes to washing-up.
Joan makes her face up.
Jill brews up for drivers on the hob.
All feel well-chuffed for *Roger*, his choice
bowl straight at the *Jack*. All but bar *Mick*
who might be drunk and half-way sick,
a good bit bitten by he should have won, cross
not to have come first: He sees his *Spirit*
is the Ghost that Lost its Voice.

Mick sinks in *Lull* with *Lub*
who drains the *Mug* and *Sobs.*
His *Grig* seems to have lost its *Giggle*
down the *Grid.* His Glum Wits felt as frail,
as fallen through the basement of
a sunken mill to soak with *Jenny Greenteeth*
in a muddled null of puddled mossy mould, industrial.
I've never seen a pastoral that looked so dull.

Hob groans, he should be home to grow
his long-attenuated *Tang* for comfort.
Here no thing'll tingle him.
    Hick sticks his sticks in lumps of dampish sand
as if to say, *Pudding and Pie! This Odd Existence, I*
and my poor bucket! Guess who won
the shouting match twixt *Loud* and *Dumb?*.
Thick may feel *Proud* but chuck it in
a *Plop* into the ponded scum or skim
a stone over the leaden sea.
    Yon sleepers could be stifled
in a lack of noise like this but for the slapping rough-cast
from a bucket with a trowel, on the wall.
    More bad ideas get stranded in the bin.

Jack interjects his head:
It just pops in aslant across a door:
"Hey up lad *Mick,* thou looks so badly,
like thy mother's mangled laundry drooped along
the wash-house floor. You should have seen me in
the poetry of *Roger Langley,* hanging out
with washing in a drying wind, or making up
wee selves within a veritable
scientific botany of verbiage
    or *Flora* of the mind."

Hodge hedges what so ever V*etches,*
Clovers even under C*leavers,* calling
Milkmaids Lady's Smock in richer ditches
sprouting *Cresses, Stitchwort* meaning
    far more words than thought
to water your *Wild Parsley, Hogweed, Parsnip,*
under-widths of all the *Umbelliferae*
with hay-shades in the shed where *Hedge*
takes *Bedstraw, Mustard, Parsley: Parsley!*
who so well combines
    the hooked fruit spines with hairy style,
and petty *Spurges* exhibit their glands and horns;
where *Honeysuckle* sucks up *Rowan,* and the *Woodbine*
look enthralled with *Aquilegia,* as columbined
with *Jack the Hedge* as *Garlic Mustard*
doing herbal-verbal flustered says quite bold
that *Spirits* seasonally rise and fail though
lagging *Bindweed's* ever yet entrailed
about the lovely *Crumbling Fold* of *Running Wild.*

Postscript

What᷍s that I read? Is Hodge
The Master dead? I thought I heard
what Peter Riley said rise from a simper
to a wail, and thought I saw the bird-like
spirit-imp of mischief, Man Jack ipse, sat
upon a doorstep with a spotted handkerchief
before his face, and a discarded hat.
   How could a heart like Roger's fail
with such a knave as Jack to set the pace?
The case is grave, and yet it's not too glib to state
that through observant wit, throughout the poetry
of R.F. Langley, the spirit lives.

The Quiet Works

The quiet works a treat. The water treatment works
through falling steps in placid air
on quiet walks by high top reservoir.
　　Aqueous eases
as a stallion stales in puddled mud.

A mare for me for equine equanimity
on flat slack hope, by small worth mere,
down rake head stair,
　　into a vale of deep deep air
　　love brooks despair.
I be prepared to de-aspire, no more
perspiring pair, no flood of hair,
no mind to mate or hope to share
the quiet works in disrepair.
　　Love brooks the falls endure.

Wet heat, the acid moor, peat sweat
　　is sourly sweet, before down-pour
whose gushes lust to groove the grove
in rushes. Puddles sate the graven delf.

Evacuate what must. Why can't I
　　disabuse myself, of lust?

Come off in downfall, outfall, service usages
assuaged in sewage.
    Abstract issues from the surface
pipes and leaks, the sikes, the becks, the burns.
The bare clough well head springs induce
themselves through quartered arms.
    A quiet motor moves, a solemn rotor turns
a slow swish carousel around a concrete drum
of gravel. Water travels through the mill to filter.
    Working strips the water figures
down to naked dress.

Indigo running from the works, slips through
        into the clatter,
voicing sources from course's flow.
Poor lad! What is the matter?

Disquieted poor lover stumbles in defeat
as yelping plover tips the tumbril, tumbles
from a troubled youth in mill-shed fumbles
through to elder's umbral gloom and grumbles
where the waters meet in derelicted darkness,
at a confluence of brooks: the spill of self disgorged
where goit-wall crumbles into streaming turmoil.

The quiet works thought to affirm a calm
but fiction, effervescent, fetches up a storm.
    The billowed rooks over the bluff of oaken cliff
fall back to pick
    the rich green fields of high worth farm.

Clock on. Clock off.
I went to quiet works on time, with poetry to paste.
I filled some jars with compound metaphoric glycerine
and mixed ecstatic graces in with mild disgrace
at the excesses, and sad intercourses past.

    Brush up the flue. Shrug off the superfluity.
Exude the sublimate of waste. Ejaculate
ephemerality. Come off a seed-head puff.
Then lay thy own self's lime across dry moss.
    And there I got laid off.

From long hard work on soft love song I broke and took
the wrong way down from rough top edge to landspit tongue.
    The sike-spate sates the brook in flux,
        light smacks as lips unstick.
My lover's mouth
is like a scrub of birches and a rivulet debouch.

Lit violet the eye-screen, blind bright lids
    electric splits as sprit touches. Rivers
torn to shreds on rocky falls.

The real kisses were far less solipsistic.
Unreal as well the glum dub down the meadow bottoms.
Banking lapwings really wring the brain.
The spirit burns up bracken rough
    slips from the brink,
    dips for a drink
in a dark public house, in a forest of rain;
takes time to think of loving twists in nigh-on pain.
Come out, sweet art, in slapstick!

Lift up thy linen smock my love
and let me breathe on thee.
This would be quiet work.

Roll down thy tights, my gentle heart:
and let us introduce the gist to the
original vaginal ginnel, surreptitiously
in laps and slaps, light-sounding slurps
the elasticity of lips.

I drop a shilling in the old tin box. Switch on
the works. Electric flashing fuses cracks.
    Night blooms in colours of a thistle.
Night-shirts clap along a line of washing strung
beneath the moon, between the back-to-backs.

    That line unstrung, unwinding springs
undress their things, to jig and sing with
an accordion of folk. Pitch up to whistle.
Crack an old arcadian erection joke.

The pump to pull is like to draw
    the froth off life in lather-water.
Let lunar slicks lie out aslant with silver swart.
I'd rather draw amorousness in heather
    with the liquid, off the moor.

One morning after storm I went to see
    if quiet works in dream.
The goit-side wall, it seemed
    was all caved in.
The gorge had scoured a cavern in my groin.
My lower limbs disjoined. I must be celibate
    from here on out, I moaned.

I get no signal from the ginnel under shadow lee
so climb back up by high worth fields to hear and see
the flapping peewits crying through an obfuscated dusk,
the croaks of roosting rooks
    on one last billow up
just as a last shaft lights the glassy backs of feather,
black and silver quiver in a sudden sylvan spill.

Could be my last recession. There are
fewer churnings up the forest road.
Nobody almost found redundant spooks at home.

Two party ghosts are coupling
in the moonlight by a parlour fire. The lunar slicks
the shades of flame across their backs.
My creeping self gives rise to ivy up an oaken trunk;
    turns serpentine with orifice and tail;
goes like a slow-worm, with the bell-strokes
down by gradient in gear;
    then plunges up in clumping boots to land
a fine plantation on the brow with peaking larks
in a climactical sensation: sky above
    and reservoir in peace below.

Lingers with a little wriggle,
    furbelow for
    flounce and ruffle, fore
and aft before re-springing
    coital song.

When boggart springs run over ground,
when leaking hills with trickle sound,
when flapping whiteness cries aloud,
    Impulsive Lover, Pleasure Me!
The pea-wit leaps and flaps about
    the old mill goit, for it
attracts him as a rhyme does to a poet.

A time-spill marks the site of quiet works.
Time spent listening for rivers
    as if ears were apertures to sapience,
as who can hear the sprouting sycamore for
    rising sapling,
or the wood shed rot spread over earthen grass,
the falls of elder florets on a forest lawn.
    Within, a bout of quiet coupling
settles: the imaginary forest hall.

A copula of bogles ground
   the oracle down to the bone up bracken rough
until the silver sang with spring-line glitters,
sheen with leapings and palaver,
in the pouring rain on shaw green pasture.

She'll be the fritillary, while he does bogey
in a clump of pine.
   Together they turn wagtail,
hopping boulders on the stream in flow.

The cream-screen shows how horse-drawn clouds
cart treasure from the pits: the mutual
   assured securities of silver cloud-cover
by fan rays, floss, and flounces off.

Uncanny sounds the empty concrete shippon
   in the tumbling of a hollow churn.
The shadow bushes darken at a confluence of brooks.

I have the ghosts evicted
   from my own unsettled state.
The last I heard of them was in the clicking
   of a snicket gate.

The fictional romance is of a ruined castle,
peasantry oppressed beneath a leaden welkin
    glum and dumbly over-cast.
The goit gives off its dusky gush.
Avert from Buff the boggart, jerkin off,
    over the pit of foul-spring trough.

Celestial proof, a roof in argent float,
A field of flapping leapers, and the looping
virid Picus laughing from the throat.

Troughing drips find ways to meadow bottoms
in the groin of interlocking spurs.
The long moor naze is one green snout
that tongues in forking brooks.
Drops lick the trough pit dumps. The upshot some
distraught cupidinous comeuppance.

Really any sally in the green would do
to slither with down leafless lee,
to step out dazzled, fawn or faun emerging
onto forest lawn and I'll enjoy
    melancholy
of each and all forlorn.

Rooms in ruin, skirting torn, obstructed passages,
the broken steps, the missing treads and risers,
    come out in surprises: sunlight
    by the grit-sill falls.
We found our prepositions and our pronouns jumbled.
Tumbled heaps of masonry adorn the disused yard.

I don't know who we were nor why
we held together, and I can't say who
had leaned a ladder in the moonlight
on an ivy-covered wall. A beam slipped in the hall.
A roof caved in. A gate fell back in weeds and saplings
    in the quiet works yard.

    The Lost Arcade Entrance
    Three Pence.
    All Quiet Works On Show.

Prestidigitation offers no change from a shilling:
Vanished in a mouth-puff from the fingers sent,
the balance spent, as spelled in pigeon clatter,
handkerchiefs on strings, more flutter,
funny habits fetched up from beneath the hat.
    I saw no art in that.

Evacuate the stalls, post the finale,
before morning curtain lifts its curlew calls.
Eschew the sexes, spit the cud of pronouns,
personal, and jumbled prepositions. View
is where the Stupor takes its Pew.

I liked the art of blue gone swart.
I grimaced at them grinding oracles
    down to the bone. I groaned at his
grand stand against the grind-stone.
    One likes the way the poet took
a column of words for a walk in the park,
instructing everyone about the seepage spots along the way.
Another does object to the great clumps of pine.
I loved, myself, the soul-thing by the goit alone.
You thought we ought to just forget obstructed passages
and broken steps, and all such bogey-traps.
They only drop us in some unimaginable deeps.
I think the poet only wants to piss and fall asleep.

Flowering gorse had prickled up the forked nose.
It yellows well the twinning brook-bank mounds.
    I'll drink the bare clough mouth
and listen to the dream-speak spout:

Speak no Conjugal Ease.
Me No More Bed Abroad.
Decelerate the Plate.
Sarcastic Rooks Forsake.
No Pining Clump to Mate.

Come by the way the willow celibate takes walks.
by meadow holmes to stepping stones.
Come off, a liquid soul in confluence and osculation,
waters' meetings and the washing off the rocks.

The water treatment works. By mill clough brook
the human hum of a machine throbs deep.
The lodge calls home her ducks and geese
through humble hills to lake-like scenes
where quiet works through simple stillness
and I acquiesce

and pass by celibate; take steps to peep
into the prospect of perpetual decease;
admire defuncted heaps and rusted passions
of the once-unquiet works,
as I pass on
the question of an aqueous unrest in peace.

Three Discontinual Songs

Untroubled sang the laverock,
    a leverage of ages
trebled over skirts of waste
    untrammelled, loft in stages.

Trepid scaling trammels, hobbled
    by impediments at each rung up
into sky-written scribble:
    loft in speech.

Shy vespers breathing hay, not left
but ushered off invisibly, and not
aetheric either, nor so soft
as fluff up flue of fire,
    but fairly still as rafter dust:
the gift of fungus must.

It's not the soul out on the hill but just
a shawl that drifts
    across a shoulder of the heights
drapes fold and croft, shows bright
the breast, a bank of misted lights,
    and this excites daft fairy vision.
Eyes are shy as the revision writes:
Trains haunt the vale. Rain enters from the west.

Wild geese of art! Ghost nurses used to
tender alms in the sepulchral park. They'd not refuse to
pull us off the brink in inky dark.
My verse at best is mostly frivolously
written for a lark on clattering edge. Nonsensical
the sentences, as the recorder notes,
flout scale in court ensemble. Images
are put to shame in false resemblance. Worst is
scrambled warble such as fails to charm
　　or salve or calm the qualms
by fair revision: Pitiful the plaintiff verses
　　of poetic plight! The verbal thrills
sound hollow over flat and height. From hills
the earthbound curses follow all the birds in sight.

Cue swallow sweeping through the shining buffets of delight!
A brash black ousel taking flight
　　from birken scrub. Rook soar
above sheen shaw. Lapwing
rebounds around about the green head spring.
More hushed, a dipper forages the disused lodge. Then loud
a treeful of successful chaffinches. More proud,
a kestrel idles in the wings for ages.
　　Then upstaged
by young and wee cock-jenny genuinely spinning wren.

Jenny trots in cavernous awareness
down a carnal alley to a tavern in Avernus:
    It was the first Free Festival of Bacteria
ever held in the Mouth of Decay.
The lanes are filled with parked cars. The acts
are drawing lots. And in poor jenny trots
to stardom: shilly-shallying
    with sheer agility. Her fancy parts
get tarted up. The show is taffeta
and laverock: the stricken soul
filmed in arcade façade.
    She did a sad ballad.

That shawl again. The shoulder drape
wrapped for the draught.
    The fire a heap of damp subsiding
to a droop between a lifted kirtle
and a lavatory cock. It could be plaid
against the brick-work of back
    paradise street lost,
without flame, without progeny, without
soul, sleep, hope, but cold as frost and deep.

I pissed upon the burning plot
of stars and out pure jenny trots.

Three More Discontinual Songs

No shades to draw but pin a sheet to rotten frame.
  Poor glazing and a broken pane.
The wind and rain broke in at dawn.

I slept with an imaginary poem. Sally greenwood
was her name. I loved the warmth
  of her imaginary blood. We both were snowbound
up by hollin wood throughout the storm. It's her
imaginary breathing keeps the phantom body warm,
but when I called her sally greenwood she was gone.

All growth died back. Grey broken cloud.
Fresh sleet. A blanket blanked whatever moon.
Black evergreen, dark holly bank.
  The cloud foreclosed,
and no more shadows show
  her absence by the gate in snow.

I long hung out in passages
  of passing time: a figure
in the passage to the door. Snow thaws
  to flying sleet and dirty earth.
The given time is given time. The
  passing time is passing.
She was a lovely poem, all unclothed
  although her heart, the very hearth
I failed to light a fire in, damp and cold.
  We wanted curtains
for a drawing to the close.

Inert in earth, the frozen dead await revival
under snow. Sun lights the icy silence
    and the cold is thrilled. The tinkles glow but,
as it overclouded, hapless goblets
are left unfulfilled, are carelessly discarded
as the spirits leave the show.

Robin sips the drops from an icicle tip
depending from a face of grit.
    A case of the election of delight
in chance clear frissons,
    a clairvoyance: the unfrozen unforeseen.

If I'm not dreaming then I might be mad but
I thought I might have been hearing here the
talk of the dead, and one was boring in my head
for ages how it really was that they had not been
angels, that were never dancing, and not on some
lumpy hob, but on the end, the tail, the tang
in the infinite tip of a single tiny pin, but they were what
we dead call fairy folk, now all gone in
for warmth and music, rounds of
    minuet and violin,
down in the mound they play within.

I think I rather think I'm happy to be left among
platonic delicates, grape wine and gala cakes
for catering. Could I have stayed and heard
the cackling becks, I might have spun, twined, turned
some fine conglomerated silicates to song.

What are these uncleared images still here for? What
are they thirsting for? I guess some lissom spring
to blossom from a pip of crabtree core. How is that
figure twixt the shippon and the midden called,
    half-hidden as the shadow falls?
What muzzle tips a tap to let an airy gush
swish in the iron manger dish of mistal stall?
    A gang of bestial images range pastoral
out on a mission up a moor.
    What are they meaning for?

Forked lyric piteously barely fit to fake
a made-up world for local gentry in a private park
and call it rough edge poetry
of squalid villages about the mills, the grime
of scabby hills, of cakes of coal
and iron, grit and building-sand and lime,
export exploits, the boiling stacks across the plain,
the bankrupt works, the closing mind, the failing mine.

O Holy Bank of Halliwell in Heaven
or in Living Hell! I woke up where the motor fell
into bank-bottom muck: stuck down by willow brook.
And who will sally forth and pull me off this time?
    A tractor motor in the wood starts up.
Great haunches gather traction through the boggy glade.
Above us billow rook. And wren and robin
    chirp with rhyme. She purrs just like a bird.
At last we melt retraction
    into sweet salacious slime.

Old Lad

Old adam, widower of croft fold farm, nab gate,
doffs rags before the living eve of death, and laughs:
Those heaving thighs, that quickened breath
    and the enormous sighs unsettle rafter-dust
that drifts to stalls for beasts long since deceased;
He lies in laithe-loft hay-must.
    Ghost-mistress eases off his clogs.

Adust: Archaic, dry, outworn. The term survives
in written form. So may the tree be seen
depetalated by a summer storm, and later on
deleafed: A writhen thorn.
    Moss rags blow off the roof.

How paradise is lost in cowardice through married life
is daft. He waited while the oaken purlin bent
under a weight of grey stone slate until it broke.
The load was pitched into a heap. The nettles grew
and turf encroached. Unspoken for, the toppled stone
    depletes by theft without complaint.
From footings elder shoots to fruit.
    Croft fold collapse, forever incomplete.

In poetry the lines portraying impotence
must have to fail. The times on common heath or bent
with insects winging in to sting the sweated skin
within sweet hairs and sticky interstices have become
the pangs, the bites, the tunes of small-importance songs,
kept in a keepsake box of doorless keys
and unadopted coinages, as *pulchral* for
the breasts. You'd need a wrecking bar
or jemmy wrench to prise open that chest.

That's her sat here, some jenny, pulchral in the couch
just in a slip. She draws by hand her ankles in
to raise the knees and show the wrinkled rose below
her puckered nose. And that's her No, and her
     entire satire.

Old lad survives his inquisition on misogyny,
her promiscuity and gross attire, her milking plump
at pastoral stool, and in her flying rags:
     She skirts the caverns of the earth with
broom and birch, swabs steps with mop, tips slops
into the ditch. Old lad sleeps wetly with the *mollyblobs*.

Scratting naked earth for the surviving words is *poultryscrawn*.
The old lad down the risers treads the steps and so they bent.
Felt cord or worsted in the legs,
    he clogs up under edge. At stairwell springs
into his throat the lump of things gone wrong.

Old doffer lost his bobbin in the lodge.
A cloud of drizzle drifted past. Drain clogs again *disusage*.
Fungoid walls melt into heritage.

Drizzle lingers in the parlour half asleep.
    And not but what some old constructions don't
entirely disappear, but linger, as do
negatives of yesteryear, odd little tricks
    and turns of atmosphere,
as here he hung his coat up on the door,
and there the tractor sunk in alder carr.

Roofdrops tinker on some castaway enamel.
Drizzle on a field of animals. The clough nook hole
soaks damp while sun breaks out in sweat.
There drizzle drifted off: He strays his steps:
    A long wet tramp into the swamp.

The old lad frozen to a standing stone:
    His ghost is at his wake.

Come in lad, with the coal-bucket
and clanging fire-irons. Bring the scuttle to
the inner parlour. Never mind alarms.

They were clearing cloud and flying rags
by day and night. By daylight they flew kites.

The midnight saw them in the moonlight sharply antic
while it soon reclouds and things retract
        into their shadow space.

        Hanging verse in space,
the pennants of a comico-pathetic reciprocity,

cantankerous as misfit,
inherent collapse, in rags of song.

Come in here as toast: The Poetry of Silence
in the parlour with a glass, in The Sepulchral Arms
under Barren Edge. And never mind the sirens.

What I Do Mean

I did mean dwellings in the dripping rain,
old meanings, old outlying farms and rotting cars,
scrap yards and overclouded brooks, and so I went
to take a look at what I might have meant by
sometimes rummaging in books about
how nellie longarms used to take us down
the astley brook, but I don't really mean
she took my soul there, so I took back
the rebuke. I neither really meant to either
come down on old jenny greenteeth in
the ponded scum, nor puke. But the rebuke was really
that I cast too many lines of shilly-shally,
shaly coal and melancholia, all too much laced with
frilly solace. This is not a laughing matter
but an anaesthetic joke about the state of water
and the fake of feeling bitter about lancashire and here
I'll draw a pier and we can almost hear along the coast
the most idyllic funfair from afar.

I might have meant how the face of a place
as it was may remain as a ghost when it's gone.
The yards and hovels of back progress street
that backed on prospect mills are lost. Witness
for instance how the name remains. The little lane
became an access to the carpark of a mosque.
The porous brick already crumbled when at last
they pulled them, humble dwellings, down. The site is
just up from the traffic lights, and not far
out of town. The ghost of this
on wider screen has ridden waves
of cotton trade, slump slums and slang slung in
a wicker creel of rotting bobbins. In language
the recycled squalor can be turned to song
with brick tanks full of water
and a cooling tower that looms up where it stood:
Another ghost, another face quite near the place
where astley brook finds confluence with river tonge.

The grey souls pooling by the soakaway
had never gone away. These figures for
their spiritual expenses, outerwear for their more
inner journey, never did add up enough
to fill a rising hole. Tin coats their can.
They can no longer hold or drink their sense of sin.
Some slim slips, disinvested cotton, slump
into the swamp of bogpan bin.
And there I thought I saw in some
damp patch the figure of a man with some
damp matches in a damper jacket pocket
sensing what it might be like
to have been damned. It could be worse. He cannot catch
the light of heaven nor ignite
the fires of hell, or nor yet burn the damned mill
down to the ground in time for it
to be demolished. I can see how lost souls stream
from the theology to future verse, industrially polished.

A whole hillside of ghosts had gathered
round the parlour fire and I began
to tell a tale about my fall.
It was falling dark on a wednesday night
in a dark public house, in a forest of rain.
In fear of the dark at the top of the stairs
I turned. I had thought better of it. Friday
morning saw me ganged up with dull spirits
hauling ropes to tow a sinking overloaded boat
along the cut. I'd fallen in with that.
I had some thoughts in coal geology about it all.
Could not the poets re-invent the soul
and re-decorate, recalibrate, heaven and hell?
The pit was burning up on hades hill. As well
imagine rochdale water grove. That cheers me
by the fire with ghosts departing thoughtfully but
hopefully as puzzled by the sleight rhetorical solution
as myself, unsolved, disclothed. I can no more this tell.

A Round Word: World

The world is too large to be held in a word,
too multifarious in meanings and too vaguely blurred
for a tune to be heard or a tale to be told.
But the word, the *world* is surely roundly globed
as an orb, or ringed in a circle
    as the kingcup sepal whorl of marigold.
A world is absorbed in the woods, in the words
for an earthen mould. It's the word
    not the world that is dense as the brain
in the bone-dome home of my own.
I do like to explore my mental limits. Happily
they're close at hand. Among simple words
there is a happy land for dimwits where
the world is fair. Its field is shared and varies
in exchange with deals in equity and folk and fairies.
Here for sale at stalls are idiotic coinages
as *bonnified*, a bona fide arcadia
of pastel beauty pastorally shown along with
the associated dairies. And indeed
I have myself the world personified as
all my care is for a world as mad
    as John Clare had for Marys.

The waxing year upsprung in either hemisphere,
full-breasted world! Undressed
as a cumberland wrestler, bosoms cradled,
nestled in her folded arms and partly veiled
by either flaxen or by sable raven hair,
the elbows resting on a trestle-table. This her stall
displaying all the pulchritude of ample blossom,
pots and jars for charity or profit, floral,
    verbal, choral, all for sale on gala day,
among beribboned shires and all a dale's regalia.
The band play shining buffets in the windy buff,
their brassy air-blown tunes go drifting off
among balloons and drifting sally fluff.
Fell runners puff to track and trail the crags above.
The county set in tweeds today I nearly love:
A sort of failure, falling into guff and tory
country stuff, with stirks and yowes
for sale or prizes, and a whirling well
that rises at hill foot. She gushes horizontal.
Pumps and trumpets steal the show.
The world's well-swollen tump: A Trump:
    The beautiful full frontal.

Half-way through the world, perhaps we might begin with
how to start, and you can draw your own conclusions.
You say a world is any apprehended whole, and that
the widest world is far too large for us poor moles
to dig or feel at home in, and suppose you can
rhyme that with *roaming*. This is no
creative writing lesson. You may drop your tone.
I'm saying this. I saw the horse-drawn clouds on gala day
got blown away, and it was then I felt
the well-rounded world beneath my feet
roll as a ball, and teetered off it.
There are far too many meanings of the world
to rhyme things with for profit. Half-way through
I turn to more secluded walks up sheen wood shaw.
Mill lodge. A mass of golden saxifrage. An empty stall.
The spring well hid. I come up wordless
from bank bottom to bare floor. Concrete
and scattered glass. The boarded inn.
Some scraggy grass. It seems the fair was over.
It was over there. So sometimes wordlessly
I'll walk a world of holes
and significant pitfalls. Spoil heaps. Shaly coal.

And once I would be wordless curled
inside a world-deflated ball,
    who would have much preferred
to never have been written or personified at all,
but as a worthless child in tears about the unfair world.
With mother-all he'll never now be unified
with bugger all but see her needy as a she-ghost
of the wordy world. So wordless talks: I don't see why
she need be shy before my scorn. What did her
trestle table ever bear? It only bore
some poor sepulchral ware. I got told off
for talking there, and feel ashamed for her.
A barer and more worthless stall I never saw,
and all she sold was space to let for hire,
a vesture proof against the water-spirits
of a watershedded shire. I'll say no more.
I came in at the end of the wake for the death
of the fair. No fun; no fanfare, but some
overclouded stalls, and darkened down the cinder lane,
the bluebell spinney, making for a mental,
fundamental, space of gesture: wording phrases
in a shady world, the worldly shade of sycamore.

PART TWO

(16/2/2017)

Scaplings, Star Jelly,
and a Seeming Sense of Soul

1

The edifice of work and life, an old retaining wall
that long held back a seam of flaking shale
collapses as a crumpled face into a rubble pile.

From high imperium to small importance fall
impotence, imprudence, impertinence and all
the way from imputation back to impact
trail the files for miles and fail
for want of style to face the facts beyond recall.

Nobody floats his boat about to clear
the fogbound coast of panacea. Nobody steers
his craft across the shoals of an obscure idea.
Nobody hears the siren singing as she sorts the shells
from shingle on the pebble shelf. Nobody tingles quite so well
the singularities of english as myself, I've seen me swell.

The sky turns bluely black to blackly blue and back.
The forky bolt ignipotent shot over scroggy holt,
a blitz illumination, a synaptic jolt,
a stroke of light to startle coney in the delfstone delf.

2

The thunder follows on through bright alarm to rumble on
through the amorphous hollows, training rain
to riddle issues through to quench and douse
the sparkler in the brain and calm the furry bunnies in the stony
coney-warren of a muddled brain, the funny farm.

These petty strokes leave clapping echoes strewn
across the green of a disclouded dream of flapping
pants and singlets dripping from a line of song,
and wraiths of steam arising from the rushes after flood.
Wet paths of mud gleam through the spring clough wood.

Air clears to seeming sweet and clean.
There's something being done down smithy dene:
a smitten smatter, spatter, clatterings
of engineering doings down a smoky sylvan scene.

Poor old potbelly fails to heat ramshackled shed.
Gobspit frazzles on the hob. Steam-engine
throbs to sobs and idles, stammers, stutters
to a stop quite dead in sullen sudden silence. Still
soft water sidles up to slip the sill of grit.
Her ripples tipple on the lip and fall down clough hole pit.

3

Gobspit was lowlife, word a worm
for earth and slime, and sly in love
with sally fluff and becky clough. He'd
had enough of milly grindrod in the engine shed
and being ground to swarf before her wanting more
out of the ore. He'd be a sapper or a mining mole
deep in a hole and frotting hills
of earthen froth up, nothing mouthing but a grubbing in the soil.

Am I not for a higher, more
respectably poetic tone? The poet calls
the lark a laverock and not a lavatory cock.
I labour with a breathing feathered heart that is my own.

Pronounce selected t's as glottal stops.
Gobspit emits from throat the spirit spots,
The cherry pops its shots, its pits it spits.

And there it sits out on the tongue-tip spit,
that little bit of silicated grit. In light
it glitters in infinity. The soul is reconciled to loving gobspit,
and their wedding train leaves long tang litter, well-worn
beck and calling in the milk of misty morn.

4

Gob's thought is working on the job while mixing mortar
made of sand cement and water on a board by shovel
all by hand. The body that's the thought of matter
sought to not so badly but to better split infinitives
to slivers, slices, silvery with mica flakes and niceties of grammar.
Thought of matter took up chisel and lump hammer for to clump
obdurate lumps of grit for scaplings, which are little shapes
to wedge and flush-up perfectly the wall-face
of the gritstone blocks. There's use for odd redundant rocks.
Thought takes a break from thinking in the shining dazzle,
muscled effort, rising, sinking, singing in the sounding rings
of steel on stone. Clouds gather round the great sky basin dome.

Thought's break is broken by a call for scaplings from the bloke
up on the scaffold, lugs a bucket of some chosen shapes
upladder, gives the handle to the mason in his apron.
Dougie Robbins sets his blocks on composition, finds a pinion
to his liking, nods approval to his novice of a mate.
The scapling is inserted. Dougie taps the block on top
by trowel. Happily it settles on its mortar bed. Doug Robbins
smoked Capstan Full Strength all day. The cancer took his throat
and now he's dead. His walls'll stand for centuries up high field head.

5

The sand is sand from crushed sand-stone. The water's from the trough
set in the intake wall. Cement is from the cement store.
The blocks: not writer's blocks but good kinderscout grit.
The sound is sound and thought a sort of mortar.
As for scaplings there's a litter at your feet of small iambic
and dactylic shapes set face on paper as a fit, a lyric feat for feet
or forfeit. Sit here on this stoop and wait to meet a bogey at the gate
or some not someone far fay lighter, flightier, alliteratively
fluttering the tapes, or you may greet some no thing frotting groans
in vapour of the passing clouds. The throat wings quails and peewits
as the pips turn blue, or so a flautist fellow saw his soul
seduced in youth by flatteries of a fellationist or two.

A boy says to his muse O you are so pronounced round,
willow, will you, wilt thou now get to grips,
distend thy lips upon this imp of little wit, a glittering
of quartz and little bits of silica in grit. There stood a spirit,
mica sitting up the tip with broken crockery and a discarded pan.
There was a man whose soul sprung from his long protended prong
as he remembers this is what I was I am, so long on truth
but not so thick, so wick a prick, he thinks that there was bliss in this.
It sat upon the thrilling point of graining streams. It would be pain
to be refused. The muse says in your dreams.

6

The old mill by the stream down ellen dene no longer
screeches with machines. From wheel and water, coal and water
burning off to steam for cotton. Bobbins all got doffed. Then steel
was milled for motor parts. Still valley streams. No turbines now
disturb the scene. The ghosts are keening not to get forgotten. A shell
of stone gathers its moss. A sunk tank fills with sediment, with alder,
kingcup, saxifrage, a picturesque of heritage of the industrial age
and locus for some psychic delectation, snap for a repast
with ghosts of workers clogging up the path back from the past.

Dark clouds brook mill. A floor of flags that's carpeted with celandine
remains a spot of colden since the olden times, secular ground
made sacrament in image. Time seems to gleam with stains of dream.

A ruinous eyesore becomes an asset, fit for sketch or photograph
by phone. I saw a vegetative growth cover the facets of the stone.
Stepped into a dripping cellar one finds pleasure in this grot:
A stinking tank filled with the thrills of mating frogs;
a sump of base desires. The boggart sits beside us here.
I drink my bottled beer up on the bank, by the remains
of broken drains, the pits of long-extinguished fires.
A floral colour leaks its inks across the page. I feel my age.
The muse looks handsome drinking wet white wine in rain.

7

The raucous bell breaks on the ear: Teabreak! It falls to me
to stop the belt. The switch is red. I have to climb a little ladder
to switch off repulse fm. A silence spreads across the shopfloor
of the shed, a foretaste of the peace of heaven when you're dead.
The sweet tea tastes eternally ephemeral as fairy cake,
a light confection, as to play is like to laik, as plea is pleased
to plead for pleasure, prayer for the revenue, unmeasured praise
in reverie, a sheer lake glade, a risen rose, a misted
forest mere, the sheerly immaterial, the animal a soul,
a blooming luminosity of vapour shot with light from up above.

A shining scene shone through the break, ten minutesworth
of timelessness is all that heaven takes. Too soon electric
raucousness disrupts our midday moon. They do our souls
a moral wrong. Please wake us from our break with softer gong.

Back on us heads along the line we match and sort things,
broken images, the rusted bracken beds, the busted heads
and rags of rhyme, the suits and ties, the curlews, peewits, larks,
the bandstand bands in proud municipal parks who blew
loud tunes unto the clouds, the merry lark recorder quotes
re-ordered notes. A single tonic rings a tingle sonic. Clinks in drink.
Sinks in the sea. Sandpiper, sanderling in ripe riparian disorder.

8

The spring winds down, the wood winds down around phonetic lanes.
The klaxon sounds a horn lugubrious, less dryad now more druids
doing dark deeds in dusky woods. In open fields above
the peewits flap with rainclouds overlapping crying echoes
in the brain for love, come out for nought but doubt.

One had been ushered out discourteously for clownish rude
discordances and audience offences, flirtatious flouncy flippancies
and fripperies and flatteries, fatuities, or at an utter
stuttered mutter of provisos and perhapses, as the ripple tipples
at the falls to lapses and collapses, and the flow is run to waste
in long protracted flaws of fluency and taste. To putter out
with bees in buzz, with furze in fuzz, drummed out by snipe,
piped down the street with dinner pans, beclouded, disenlightened.

Subject to fright, subject took flight at depth, as death is
first suspect, heart subject to arrest, the spirit figure of the soul
benighted and by dolour exejected, abject
throwing up and giving over on the edge of passing out.

One two feet deep in sphagnum stood for sad defeat. Wet moods
of sally woods, her effluent a trickle down green gowan gown,
the peat soil slit rush spilt with spoil. A dribble spouts turmoil of soul.

9

If soil be soul and sediment be sentiment, then mood be mud
lumbrilical and umber and the word be worm and warm in worn-out
slumber, and the corpse be copse if death has no more depth
than grave delusion, then let language languish in an anguish
sandwich. One is undistinguished and the other
gets extinguished in the gut. One is a number, and we can't be sure
if nought be one or not. Rhythm goes dumb and dumb be dumber.

Sunk in deeps the inward word-wood, sunlit bogs of glassy lucence
and assailed by some elusive sibilance of eructation, gasps of gas
let slip emit in hissy fits, the ghost is given up like burning flakes
of paper or the broken bits of gift, refused as if returned to sender.
When a soul is born it must at once be given unto universal gender.
A soul is but a noun however buttered up and better
disengendered. Anima is fitter, grander, as a lovely lass,
for lad a lover, self his other. She is april in a flowered apron.
She is shepherdess of trespasses up at the reservoir. She is
the egregious head of a flock of woolly fools, the old
souls of the dead who scratched initials in a wooden board
at school. The cloud sun shadows pattern o'er a moor.
Lad law stone stood out up on a glaciated peneplain, a dunce on stool.
The outcrop fingers rump hump tump lump, the prone pennine,
along the spine, anima turns nook hole supine, a sauce for gander.

10

Abed I take the weight supine, the feel of gravity in space and time,
the physics of impressment on a mattress, and the grace of being
in the abstract as a concrete base of life on earth
compressed by backside and by spine. I blame the weight of time
for my decline. My brain's not quite without my mind. Give time
the time to time the rise to praise being alive. It only wants
an hymn to the ossific theos in cosmology,
with binaries and dialectics in our minds before our eyes.
We shall endure immaculate the pure idea of song.

Is it not clear you can't lose a belief you've never held
but just adjust how the imagination lusts after belief
(no must without a mould aroma) and the mating melting meld
and jelled with a religion of the heart? Behold the bleeding pump
up on the cross! The fancied loss is less a grave of bells and bones
than a cremated dust. Out crop the larks with their creative thrust.

No arguing with gravity, take the advice of base mechanics.
The soul is not for being shunted with a pole into a pit
but rises to the stansfield heights from meadow bottom hole.
I bow to gravity and his implacable demonics, and the falling call
of panics at a greater cavity. It is great gravity that animates
the waters in their courses off a moor, and not depravity at all.

11

Gravity and time embrace behind cloud curtains on the rushy bed.
They wrestle but they fail to reach high knoll edge peak.
The space of mind within themselves is disassembled, depersonified.
Imagination's lust after belief is deeper and more certain
to be gratified. She takes him in and he finds room inside.
The weight beats time, their breaths abate in common sense of space
and light looks like a grace. A fine word heaven for a high blue sky,
high altocumulus and sunshine superflected their ecstatical exertion
up on a plateau, the jumps and stomps of supercelestial blues.
There was a time there was a god the weight of primal giant
liked to ply a clientele with hush in peace and mutter on the quiet.

The cave within a bramble thicket, who goes there
but smug and snug, a pair of juggled smugglers
in a landed country where the customs are corrupted by romances.
They share the contrabanded proceeds of their literary airs and fancies.
France is as they say the source of brandies as demand is
supply-source to hearty country gentry. There's a barrel
in the cellar, there are bottles both in garderobe and pantry.
All our ghosts are wisting to enlist in the historical romance,
a dance that twists true unbelievers with untrue believers,
flagstone delvers, handloom weavers, packhorse galls and border reivers,
stone posts, causeys and a list of hostelries now lost.

12

Time comes round, drained and changed, the ground estranged.
A hollow tone is bottomed out midstream in stone. The body
as abstraction but impersonates real beings in a dream
of puddled green. One clump spawns many pollhead souls
and some a heron ate. What's ground to love down to the bone
has been by blame deranged. The gouged holes have left a mound
with turf regrown, the pit backfilled with small-worth spoil
and sparsely soiled but burrowed in by bunnies on home ground.
In gravity the water falls. Space and time are barely creatural.

A seepage from the ferrous sike bleeds red, the leakage
of the heathen earth, the earthen heath, the turf herself
of heather shelf, flaight grough and high rough bent,
the ferny bracken hough and stuff, the bonny clough,
the claypit greaves, the digs of roadstone delf.

The earth has sex, unvexed and disperplexed, transgender
as a fancied elf, LGBT in robust health. Let me
be he myself: The last wet dream he'd had had had him
slipping off the saddle-back of long ridge slack and sliding
down a flood-gouged landslip bank all strewn with bulbs
of sprouting bluebells plump and pluming blooms, a blubbered roar,
orgasmic weather, as if the earth had given him what for.

13

The works of life fell slack. Blank looks the order book. The bank
bites back the debt, account foreclosed and in the red, already auditors
in black are at the gate. They look like rooks or crows
with clipboards in their claws. We stand by our machines
as they take notes. We bleat a bit at heart, facing another
firm's demise. Turned out into the street, our gate is closed. The end
of a financial year brings on fresh unemployment, and the springs
of our expenses shall be stifled, squashed to the allowance of a dole.

It's april in the afterlife and there are daffodils
down lee wood hole. A soul is spirited adrift over the ruins
spread along moor edge. It's not like heaven, more a squalid
hilltop village in the eighteen-forties than a band of angels
bright in orange light. The afterlife looks much like life before.
Death is a physical relief; geomorphology a matter of belief.

What grows and glows is roses and erosis as a weight
of water falls to riddle issues, flooding flushes
down the face of earth in spate to spout rock fissures
troughings, downpipes, gutters. Light itself I see is blind
and cannot see itself, nor feel nor fall, though not unfailing
shines on mossgreen slime from time to time. Earth quakes,
knees shake on entering the procreative evolution personal to all.

14

Yearly I've been seeing april in her flowered pasture
apron. She'd be shawled in gauze of flimsy mist.
Me being me I'd be the mimsy euphemist, she'd be so
lackadaisical with celandine, and like a daisy in a sward of grass.
I'd see her flank the flaking path down from the pass
of gatepost gap. By seeing her I mean no more than we had
not so much as kissed, though I have slept with april in a dreamy nap,
she breathing in my lap, the better bliss I missed. Her fleecy clouds
come down to nibble at the richer grass of meadow holmes.
They spread out in a riddle where the waters graze the flats.

Trunk gaining girth and height, grains bustle to a bush of streams
of clean delight. I mean like growing pains, the groans
of meet your mate, the forking point of two fine tingling tines,
twin rivers' jointure to the stem. The tree in mapped
geography's a reach from estuarine umber roots to branching
fantasies and dreams. From intake grazing at the sources, flowers
fruit in an accordance with abstracted forces, watercourses, streams.
Mathematics might describe the pattern of the paths amounting
to the springline founts, the well-head issues. Seeping seems
the spirit blood of psychic earth in ruddy blushes from the water shed,
rush mouth to sad reed bed to far sea sun set deep in bed
by runnel, barrel, tunnel, culvert, waters funnel well.

15

Run down the ruins of the works, the textual and textile history
of industry to which these cloughs gave birth. See seepages
that percolate the earth. Skip heart a beat; skip scout and leap.
Hark to the glistering of riddles in the ears, the trickles down
by hanging royd, by heather shelf, knoll edge back to myself.

Pegs in her teeth and outstretched fingers, pegging out a line
of clouts in wind: shirts, shorts and sportswear hanging out
by greenwood lee, the coloured bloomers, sheets and skirts,
the flapping nappies under squeaking peewits, croaky magpie cries,
snipe drumming from a clouded sky. That peggy's a goodlooking lass,
her heart her looking glass, her breasts beneath her vest.
She keeps a kitchen garden by the high farm yard of art.

A brownish crown of rounded ground lets down a gown
or mantle, bent and heather past its pinkish peak,
a rough sward dipping to the brink of buck stones edge
now plunges in a bank of green or rusted bracken.

Sikes leak a simple liquid to a long catchwater drain
to feed reserves for flushing, washing bodies, washing pots and pans,
to bathe in and to drink. The water in the rain is on the brain;
the water in the wind without the mind, sunshot with sudden showers.

16

I view us two that day we came along the long catchwater drain
the climate light and delicate, a touch intemperate, the weather cold.
I can't recall the exact date. The ground it seems is owned by some
consortium of infrastructure funds. When water passed
to private hands the heart deflated and evaporated from the state.

Our land miss-sold, how gently by permissive footpaths now
across their land our right to roam's controlled! Free hearts for health
and heath. The heather blossom's old. The physis that's the bios,
physics of our lungs and things we hold above the ground beneath.

You're only looking at a poem in a book about us on our way
along that long catchwater drain, we came upon, we almost slipped,
we stumbled on some clumps of a gelatinous translucent matter
in the grass beside the path beside the idle drainwater that's caught
endiked to sidle by a contour line to which the sikes all sink.

Traversing a floodriven rockslide, I was thinking of
hydrogen dioxide, and the nearest pub for drink, the malted barley,
hops and the fermenting yeast, the tides of pubs and shops advancing
to retreat. What is this stuff down at our feet on turfed peat?
Star jelly slime. It's not alive. It's not a white freed from its yolk.
They say it has no DNA: a fallen star; an old folkloric joke.

17

It was a bland but practical procedure just to look it up on Wikipedia.
I wrote some quotes of dated little notes: When I had taken up
what I supposed a fallen star I found I had been cozened by a jelly.
John Dryden 1679. Sir Walter Scott has called it foul.
I do regret I failed to smell it, or, I sniffed it not.
I lacked a paper towel. And a Platonist, called More, god wot,
called it the excrement of stars. Its proper posher name is astromyxin,
that just means the same: a jelly fallen from the stars.
I quickly scanned the little list of traces, poetry and lore and fancy fable
food for bards and antiquarians, the not-in-facts of clever poets.

Inert and flaccid. No known deoxyribonucleic acid. So
it's not like snot, but more the lifelike class of clouds and streams,
and the unseen, the far-out stars. Stuff found near brown-black rough
of bracken, bent and heather in undated weather. Found some more
on drier moor, by salter rake o'er langfield-walsden moor.
I failed to sniff that like before. The angel farts of what got shot
from the celestial arse that knocks out current astrophysic lore
to pure imaginary stars. Biologists'll sort it out I'm sure.
Astromyxin! be my image of the human soul, replacing sexed
and predatory victim vixen with a bellyful of jelly foul! It will not do
to spoon and trifle with the sweet ethereal, the spiritual matter
fluids must excrete. Is it not wet? The heat has eaten heart in sweat.

18

Envisaged is the savage face of fiction, victim, vixen.
Flayed by fangs how her fur flies! The living soul dies in her eyes.
The tears that reach her ears are merely literary airs. She's being
done to death by hounds that mug poetic diction, and the cries
evaporating to a vapour in the skies are tears in paper fabric
dampening the scribble script ripped out to foolscap paper scraps.

At death what flits is nothing that did not on earth exist
in brake nor thicket. See how quick it discoheres. Soul in solution
disappears. A lifting shade the clearing clears. Soul reappears.
The metamorphic frog spawns in a puddle of sikeriddled bog
ditched in a dike, an idle goit, the eructations of a croaking poet.
One clump equals a great amount of eggs per frog.
How few shall make it through to mate and croak! Soul were a joke
unborn, unmade and uncreate, it dies in eyes. Now see how low
dead jelly lies dead in the dead prosodic lines!
The starry glair of soul, that has nor redolence nor niff
but by surprise. If I find more star jelly, memo, take a sniff.
It only says no DNA has been as yet so far identified.

What is nor male nor female wasn't born and hasn't died.
I took this jelly for an emblem, soul-ideal self-referential,
immaterial incarnate falling flat to flat to flatter than flat joke.

19

The picture-emblem of a visionary boredom changes
from a grey seacoast to dreary moor, a heron
flapping idly o'er, and drearier abandoned works, the heartbeats
of the desperately poor, the sunken sinks, the pits that picks
have bitten into brinks for stone, the lonely feeling on your own,
sad sumps and sandstone spoil, of clay and coal, a sense
of soiling in the soul, the panic and the rising dolour, having
to bring plumbers in when living on the dole. You feel yourself
a spiritual invalid depressed by such invalid stresses, spilling messes
in a handy hole. Why bother being born when you are bound to die?
I dallied lodged on ledge above a valley for despondent years.

Escaped from deceased lover in a dark dream melodrama,
fancy rather that my soul pupated as a nymphalid,
a pili-pala quite fritillary as lily for fertility, the wings of fruit,
sweet in a metaphor, a metamorphic suit, escaping
pupillage in state, in better shape, obtect or exarate,
the object being to exonerate the earthbound bird of soul
from song in flight. The heron lifts its weight under pervasive gravity,
mere levity is left to giddy giggle fits, and just a little lift:
old ecstasy, memento, a forgotten heap, mistaken gift. Now scrub,
excoriate the fancy with a tub, abrasive vim without apology.
There was a soul that had been boggartbound in carboniferous geology.

20

The invisible worms in the visible words may squirm within
an invalid homology between the workaday world
and the demonic cobblers tampering with pins
the blethered soles. So there is no consensus
between sense and its transcendence in the fates
of faiths to fight for any temporal ascendance
as the tropes of troops fall flat from platitudinous heights.

Dull is the firmamental lull for patience waiting on and wanting
her emoluments, the rudiments of sense in expectation
of thoracic wings in the future tense. The fancy pierid
is glad just to be pupa-rid, who's grubbed in the cruciferae,
a common cabbage white in blue cerulean, the circumstanding sky.
It won't be long before the wings of song are ovulating
on the sprouts of spring. The truth and beauty thing looks bright
and not quite wrong: the grace of risen grasses and the place
a being is in space and time. The dying thing was living all along.

The meaning of the spring is clearly a mechanical escapement,
the release of tension of a coil unsprung. Now having won
my old age pension, OAP on a settee, I know proprioceptively
I'd seed no new conception so I'd not need contraception.
Birds, bees, do as ye please. I'll rest my case on knees and couch at ease.

21

About sex no-one thinks straight. Translate that axiom to latin
as a rueful saw. The rational and clean cannot quite face the messes
and obsessions, being badly innocent of sins religions revel in,
applying their repressions. Sense is bent in trying not to think about
the thing at all, the pleasure in the press suppressed. Mad youth
is up for it, to date and mate. The aged impotent half mourns
a failure to be drawn to porn, and scorns with yawns to masturbate.

Some chum at school told me that up the clough of astley brook
in barlow park there linger lasses fit to fuck, but there I found no luck.

Heterosodomitical depravity! The juice in word-abuse!
Did wings of sin fly in the casement cote on winds of some
religion like a homing pigeon? Or was it there from origin,
the apple's fall by gravity? Think straight. I don't have no opinion but
if god existed he'd recoil from his creation. He'd have been disgusted.

She crawls across the carpet from the gasfire to undo my pants.
I swoon before the prospect of a lissom onanism: rank wank produce,
a yankish jissom. And she does seem to appreciate my stand
all rubicund, robust and grand, as fit to bust, fulfilled by mouth:
Confessio! Obsessio! Fellatio! But now, oh no,
lust's lost. Do not resuscitate. About sex no-one thinks straight.

22

From highbrow knowledge down to black pit lock I have been
doing up the ruins. The disanimated soul lies as a flagstone flat.
I have been plastering lime roughing, scraping sapling ash and grass
from troughing, facing blocks with scaplings. Oak pegs grey slate
to lath. I have been pointing up above the wainsgate lane
while thinking how to cap the rimless hole that is the soul.
I have been grouting in a foetid tank until I stank and felt a chump,
a clump, a clumsy lump dumped in a sump. I sank in a morbid miasma,
shrank from kitchen squalor, sink a filthy pit of dolour. So
I headed back up to the knoll to cheer in clear, in sheer sunshine.
I feel my dear imaginary gamine anima is nearly mine.

I saw her first upon the water, shining beauty off a misted tarnface
as the gorgeous grace of forestry and fell. A prayer transpiring into air.

May springs, grasses ingress. I wander where the paths digress.
One way the ashen ghoul blanks at so many deaths: churchyards
and crematoria; ashes scattered on the river; ashes loosed in wind
up on the moor; burned up or buried. The other way is
none of this has really mattered now the sun shines and
the mountain ash is berried red. I can't as yet say earth is dead.
Mischief turned from blank misfortune to the spirit in a playful phase
of flippancy, earnest in disbelief. May springs august things back to leaf.

23

So there I stood where earth had caught a star out on the moor.
The astral gelatine lay slime in grass across the path along the drain.
Astromyxin has no truck with sex. There's no connexion twixt
the jelly and the reproductive facts. It's not attracted to by insects.
Evaporated or dissolved in heat or rain, remaining unexplained.

Fancy fancies an enhanced existence, sentenced in a trance
to sex by chance. Genetic nonsense is advanced as midges dance.
And fancy is entranced before the orificial entrance, as the chance
of fate enchants. It is for insects as it is for ants and elephants.
The secret mirth of earth secretes in knickers and from underpants.
A long disastrous providence evolves from a seductive glance.

Angels have come down in the world, as lightly or as
headlong hurled with yelps from alps of rocky physical relief.
I've mimed belief in heathen boggart of the moor, or wispy willy
over boggy carr, or slattern nelly, seductress of meadow bottom.
I've forgotten half of what I once imagined I believed in,
say a pair of guardian angels in the corner of the ceiling
watching us, a pair of innocents, just fetch each other off,
or say a vast array of jellied angels in a mass debating if
these little human blisses are all specious, spacious, gracious or
ungracious slights, the cream or scum of streams of breeding species.

24

In water as it is on earth the insectivorous amphibian
anurans meet and mate. The spawn they spawn in spotted clumps
in some abundance for insurance of genetical endurance.

The common frog's reborn in spawn, in puddles, pools and bogs.
Clouds clump in clotted lumps, in goit and lodge, in tank and sump.
The nebulae lie open to the sky, in water as it is on earth,
in leafy shade when sun is high, the weather dry, the spawn exposed
to eyes of passers-by, such as a heron gliding idly o'er
come down to ponder on a water feature, weedy in desuetude:
Ardea cinerea sees the spawn, material idea, and scoops translucent
jellied stuff from beak to gizzard. One more little drama
in the sense of life at hazard. There's a creature in the heather:
it's a lizard being spied on by a prying buzzard: pecked into the guts
in bits. Meanwhile the water sidles round buck stones and turley holes
to feed a reservoir up withens head. That could mean there'd been
sally willows sheepcropped back to the raw bent and bedrock bone.

Cloud pillows plump. The ansers bed by waters in the gorple hollows.
I who have a home drift off alone. This I is an imaginary
lonely soul, stone deaf up on a moor, a standing ladstone. Wind
whips spirit off him with a cloth. I have seen the silent spirit flutter,
flitting off among a flock of kindred flappers over airy ground.

25

The gorgeous realms of thought are like a robe of flowered sward,
a pasture, pleasant pleasure in reward as she steps free: the soul
is like a naked woman to the likes of me, my phallic fallacy
of feeling her desiring me, and she the sum and sun of one
great penis in the womb of thee and me. She stands up
in the face of them, the angels with no genitals, erect and grand,
a rubicund rubber dick end. Let her take me in hand.

This seeming sense of soul now seems unseemly, seamy
as a spent-up spoil of semen, spilled on stony ground.
True soul is seeing in the sense of feeling, meaning seeing
being yet unseen. Blindfold the soul seems kenning seeing
sound around the vision's failure. I'll absolve my soul from all
entanglements of genitalia, and so I'll button up and put to bed
this alice as a phallus in her palace in the womb entombed.

Desiring angels take the thing in hand, a stoodley pike in size.
The seed again outspilt in slime, bog eggs on th'edge
of sheer existence, symbols of a universe ensouled,
dead heads in the menstrual shed. Chill waters reach
each globe of testes, and the ferrous sike bleeds red
into the dike's reed bed. Flatulent eructation farts.
That starts an inquest on the littered corpses of the literary arts.

26

Come down in levity to ground in shame, I heard a scientific clown
on radio proclaim that gravity is not a force. His heart is in his brain.
His brain is in the stars. Celebrity's his name. That lad'll have been
boggled by his model. What he says is no help in my struggle up
the birchcliffe-wadsworth lane or midgley scout; cannot prevent
high force or cauldron snout from tumbling down in tees.
Astrophysical description translates wrongly into common tongues.
The heaven mathematical is abstract as the pastorally attic songs.

Star jelly sure is no angelical ejaculate, and yet I can't see how
the angels and the sonnet weren't there in refined potential
in the nanoseconds of the first big bang. I have such bees
in my bonnet and will freely let cosmology go hang, and hell as well.

Ghouls and ghosts and the assorted spirits take no root in
Newton's physics. The imaginary is but one of heaven's many nouns,
illiquid and unsolid. Heaven might be like a squalid moorland village
in the eighteen-forties. Bleat sheep, clack looms, trolleys rattle.
I woke up in the twenty-noughties and the digitating engineers
in technosorties had made up a perfect void. My thought is frazzled
in an abreaction to the cybernetical abstractions, conjured
out of code. I'm less annoyed by fancy prattle. Not being dead
comes after being born. Earth turns back. Sun sets before the dawn.

27

Gravestones are dated. My anticipated fate is to have been cremated
not by will. Had I a stone it should have stated: Enter Fool
Who Rings A Bell. I knew some of the bodies buried up in heptonstall.
Well you may scatter me from higher brow or you may not,
it doesn't matter what. I must not care at all about my plot.

Postmortal mind may linger in the sunlight on the water (matter)
as a living thing while overlooking tenter fields and wire works yard
as likewise tardy in retard. The water rhymes with god's own daughter,
glints on bedrock grit, its quartzy bits. A waving string, the algal slime
of life is lit and greenly shines. The dead brain cannot figure what it had
in mind. A disused mine? A song of blood that sang? Bellowing kine?
Sing coal pit spoil heap feather bed moss; shadow patches cotton grass.
Tell us a vista. Look out from up withens gate across the langfield pass.

In failing light I've written reams, rhymed streams with wetter dreams
in tender scenes that seemed to blend adhesive semen to
a cement render and it doesn't stick. I didn't think I might offend
a living soul in bonding, roughing up a cream of finish slick.
I did not intend a means to render readers sick with cream of
shaggy tupping. The failing meme ends broken down to phonemes.
I don't know why so many languages surrendered nouns to gender.
Send a spirit to the moon, and echo soon returns it to the sender.

28

From a mood in the mud in a clough in the wood to a trough
in the rough, in the sough of a wham in the hough, I blundered up
to the well head stone trough spring drain issue where I stood
perplexed at how to call the soul by text. Streams stream, flows flow,
dreams dream, blows blow. Soil soils the foot to which it clings.
A boggart left his print upon the threshold of these ruins
down clough hole, among the lumberings of other clumsy doings.
Skriking bogey rises from the cot, a dream-pit shock of private scenes.

The primal or the primate scene was one mad psychoanalytic dream.
There is mister 'aslam, father; there's my sister and my mother.
I'm another being born and feeling smothered, so I thought to scream.

I dug into a silted trough and found an antique peg for pegging cloths.
A dream-ghoul with the pegs clenched in her teeth. I called her peggy,
this must be the peg you lost back in the day when shirts were made
without their collars. You're in the works of folklore scholars. Speak!
She fades away. At home I opened up a cupboardful of moths.

The literary dome is literally made of words. The sky is occupied by
clouds and birds. Beneath the trees fly flies and flitting butterflies.
The sun sets red and gradely blues, a trigger to configurating bats,
midges and gnats. And mice and rats. A primal hunting time for cats.

29

William Blake! How often have I argued with thee in the bath! My path
by dark and stoney lanes, up to the heights has found me subject
struggling with objective facts ordained by physics and by maths
to rule the mundane shell by mathematic acts. The dome's dominion
welcomes no unqualified opinion and'll pass no measure for the force
of suction from the pit of hell but measures light quite bang to rights.
But I'll no longer meet your mad imaginations in my tub.
I took the whole suite out, bowl, sink and pedestal as well
to make a water-feature, and to grace the byclough delf with something
of myself. I have a shower so the stars may water me with tears.

They throw their spears at me in a trajectory. I've been in heaven
for a spell under the spectral bow that shows the ruined factory
below hell hole, a site that seemed to touch my soul that has been
lately dismal and refractory. It's one of them depressive-manic mills
that once abounded in our moorland hills. The arch of spears
was like a *jacio,* a throw, the reach of an expectorate,
ejaculate, a bucketful of swill upon abject, reject, self-disrespect.

Apology. I graduated from a college with small knowledge of what
frequency and wave meant. And I hadn't even heard of hymenopteran
vespology. The oakleaves fall and my imagination of the real has failed.
A scattering of spangle galls lay patterning a shining causey pavement.

30

Sheer being shone, a shining scene within mine eyes, sheer being
being humanised in phrases, sylvan green and silver sheen, sheer being
sexualised. What sex is she? I'll make a guess that light and blood
are harmonised in phases, with the wood sorrel and pasture daisies:
she: she being sheer being and coming clean and clear, a vision seen
apprised of meaning she being becoming she in the wooded ravine,
she being so becoming somewhere down luddenden dene, a sight, a site
to memorise. There's something flutters at her lips. I want to give her
literary air, with meadow bottom, head and hair and heart, clough hole
and private parts. For her I want to utter eloquence in art,
but I have butterflies at this, to kiss, to buss the blessed blooming bliss,
so I just spout what words come out to supplicate, to conquer doubt
about a poetry that's proud to be composed of flipping flippancy about
a lass no less half-dressed cantripping spells of frippery, a frilly pair
of pants for her in her wet underwear; a lad, his spirit-lamp in flare.
The pair fall down like jack and jill in tears of like teenage despair.

She is the classical opheliatic; he's scoptophiliac behind the screen
parting the rushes. They could be a paired as painted china figurines;
they could be blushes in the petals, a mayblossom bush. They could be
milkmaids and pink purslane in the ditch. But which is which?
The juicy loins, the toss-up coins, join with a spirit in the genes,
in mourning keens, cock-song for thrush-song guff of muff and gush.

31

Free grace came thrice, three graces in my life, three naked bonny
lasses splashing in the pool down three shires stone; three others,
unclothed women dipping in the water where the turvin brook
falls to the pool of jumm, below the washfold lumb. And, third,
three adolescent giggling girls, with dangling legs and scantly clothed
sat on a rock amid a little falls above a cobbled ford the water
slid across. I caught a glimpse of them from in the van, a common ford
as I was driven past. The more recall is blurred the more an image
crystallises clear: three graces as a pure female idea to which
it is as if my soul had been betrothed; my clear ideal idea
to which I am adhered. I have been once or twice or thrice adored.

Those girls'll all by now be, if not dead, post-menopausal.
Gently dip but not too deep and tell me where the images have bled.
So I went back to check my facts. Bare legs and flimsy cotton.
Clear picture of the setting. Something wetting, not to be forgotten.
Forty years on. Quite unlike. I've misremembered catlow bottoms.

I'd set them up upon a sheen of mossy stone, in silver green,
a visionary skin of living water in the falling stream. I sat
to watch each slip a sill of grit, and thought it like a dream of
elphin lucence in the light of three of them thrice over.
And only one, or two, or three of them has ever been my lover.

32

Under the influence and boggled by hypnotics of infinity, a gate
is opened onto what looks like a glade, a stage, a place to play
and deal and trade with ghosts and spirits, fay fairies and fates;
a space to laik about with mops and pails, with milking stools
and udder tits in mistall stalls and dairies. Green darkens and
imagination fails. The scene returns itself to the unseen.

In other bits of the unworldly daydream vision varies. There is
relic bones of papist saints and bloody virgin marys; there is
sacred stones, astounding the deluded fools and the antique
acidulated hairies; there are the occulted and occluding schools
for esoterica. The autotelic spirit world evolves from an america.

Come down to earth, a tufty covering on heath, a broadly
carboniferous geology. There is no space nor scope for soul's escape
from death but this benighted waste, should we neglect our rights
of way, into the glade of sheer poetical delight, instance I saw
an elfin lucence as a wish to fish from trees along the cut without
noetic licence. Stone-heart facts of matters form a block of nuisance.
Bogey squats on knoll edge outcrop rock. For poetry I'll make
splendiferous apology, new senses for the nonce. A cloth-eared satyr
plying on a rusty saw. The scholar tramps down country lanes.
A mind sees eyesore as a mine out on a moor, now mined no more.

33

A dun moor, the *I* figure bleats, my love undone, the work of ages
all gone under with the setting sun, the clamour gone with colouring
and glamour; hayfield mown to pallor and the dark night unbegun.
Come toward the end of pages. Little parts of speech have run to seed.

The lusty lads are up out and about in tractors trailing
muckspreading contraptions, spreading such rich dung out in the
drying sun and joking in among. I don't feel I am one of them.
Short dangling length gives rise and fall to weakness
of a mental strength. I do no work as such in sunshine, disinclined
to take my jerkin off. Redundancy's redundant. I have not been fired.
I am retired. I take good walks that leave me feeling tired.
I've taken wages, cash or slip. Now in the vale of love I dip
with an unpaid attention, my art is subsidised by the state pension.

The queen of may. That's one idea of florid in abundance
at the village fête. Is that not out of date? Not quite, despite
disparities of luck and fate, for if it weren't for bad luck,
an unwanted flat too deep in blues, the fate of an unlucky fuck,
there'd not be any case at all for spreading sticky verbal muck,
the dud flat notes and screeching sharps, in full gamut attack
express the drake and duck, his millpond mate, the lodge a pretty lake.
Duck dialect. Bring up by beak what's found in mud. They quake.

34

Guttural as gargoyle gurgles from the troughing to a pebble bed,
the gargle-throttle throat spouts out through teeth and tongue and lips,
the ferrous blood song sang out through rushes in the woodruff,
spouting guff in draughts of rough, to doubt redoubt in pools of hush,
and ugh how tough the gusset cleft of russet bracken clough
it is to penetrate and tup. Blood blackens where it bled. Root radical
and radish red, the tissue fissure issues, trickles rust in text and trust,
the clough hole eidolon needs must have speckled song thrush sexed.

The brain within the skull is to the mind unknown. The mind is blown
across the great outdoors, on walks out over on the moors. Recall
has been caught short of thought. Stray figures cross the waste amort.
I knew them all, wives, lovers, rivals, friends and others, all now dead
as stone gate stoops. I've seen them on the common where they pass
as ghosts. As ducks at dusk come to their dam, I do know who I am
in midgley, wadsworth, heptonstall, and stansfield on beyond.
I come down from rough heath to drink with friends at the lane ends.

By thorny ways and steep valleys young spirit goes with flows; grows
deeply fond of days and runs with long protended prong to sally in
the green wood grove along the grain, hell-bent on heaven scents.
Old 'uns abstain remembering the fiddle idylls, love in pain,
and won't go there again. Lit wick is fit to snuff, extinguished, spent.

35

Wick quickens, growth regrows; thickets thicken; birkenshaws explode
their nodes in filamental delicates from root to leaf in blue cerulean
along lines of genetic codes. A thunder showers from high heaven
to the green lungs sprung from earth beneath the flowers of the heath
all under powers gathering their lower glowers o'er the hearth,
the heart of hillfog heathen hovel home, to puddle in the peaty loam
in muddy muddle. Noises off engorged falls are shouts
of sporting boys ejaculating joys with horny ornithoptic calls.

A ghost is like a spirit that embraces place. I had been mating
in a pretty state of haze, sunshot with rays. I'd been indulged
in sheer effulgence, gorgeous floral orals in a finery arrayed
in wooden glade. The ghost mutated for a change to sour
miss peggy crabtree grimacing at the expense of pentecost. Her sallows
will all wither up at withens in the frost, and all her bairns are lost.

Fancy greenly glades the glowing stage of play on holiday.
The flats display a hill farm scrap yard. Chorus is the squealing wheels
of trolley bogeys. Dancing maids are mad for what they're made for
procreating on the moor. Cast of auditors applaud its picture sex
with claps of claque collapsed in laughter in the next
act of the text: the heaven scene of folk in a mill-village picturesque
up in the hills, blowing with smoke. If this is afterlife, it's past a joke.

36

Begin again an ending with the dinning of the tinkered pangs,
a last harangue in language of the english tongues, from hobs and tangs
to tiny tines; from grand cacophony to tinkles in fine tune
the span of sounds, a stereophany of pebbles gurgle in the streams.
I'll stick my ears out on this tongue of land, for babble sprung
of folkish songs, pastorals of the common man, the moral gabble
of a heritage of wrongs and churned up in some turbid verbal dreams.
The droning moans drown out the meanings of the nouns themselves:
the vulgar, recondite, and the improper. Nought can stop a lad like me
from drinking from it, fetching a rich vomit to a white ceramic sink.
The mucky songs of mangled flagrance got sung strangled. Prickled
is the voice of yellow gorse; the blossoms of the yellow broom.
The musky wicken and the fragrance of the bonny sweet hawthorn
add odour to a lust for place, the singularity of single singing things
like swimming in the skin where mare greave water falls into the lumb.
The muffled gongs, heptonstall bells, enthral the ears out in
the beer-yard at lane ends. With where I live I do love to be friends.

Blue air is fair. There is a heathered turf in heaven. What I saw
was more the eyesore of a squalid village in the umpteen forties.
There the wives of weavers swive so we may thrive with our bacteria
germane to gene survival. The water springs alive at rain's arrival.
Again we'll feel no pain. I'll give you this last line of life remains.

The Wooden Glade

The Wooden Glade, a phrase laid waste of pastoral
made paste of places in the past enstaged
in space: the glaze of ages fading fast,
a play displayed on gladed grass, glass cast at last
a blade made for a little lad's henrun crusade.

The wooden glade for me was made by
father's father, Edward Arthur; Haslam is our proud
surname. He made the blade a guard and
target, shield to wield: red cross on silver ground.
The proud lad had to fight the frightful cock
that ruled the wide back yard of unkempt garden

The stage a yard, back door to gate and out:
I cross the street to school, built eighty years before
for infants such as me. I had to reach the latch
and click the sneck for both reception and despatch.
The frightful cock had these, my infant calves, to catch.

A lilac tree grew up beside the gate.
The cock's pit was our patch, our pitch, and he
knew how to peck. I hang my arms up on the tree,
reach to the latch, click sneck and, out, I'm free.

I hang my arms hung up on the lilac tree that grows
beside the air-raid shelter: good red Accrington brick.
The glade of sky fills with exhaust of coal from mills.
From the back gate I cross a street of sandstone setts
to school. The playground toilets butt upon
the graveyard wall. The church is called St. Paul's.
Its spire is tall but mill chimneys are taller.
The infants' school is small but all the infants are
all smaller. Church and school and mill, these are all
tall as overlookers overlooking all. Old knockers-up
have all been made redundant. An air-raid siren
salvaged from the war's employed to wake all
Astley Bridge at six and then again at seven o'clock.

The frightful cock I saw my father give the chop
upon a wooden block one Sunday morning, and the head
fell off. The headless body ran around the yard until
it dropped. That chop had struck my little life
like lightning striking some lugubrious wooden glade.

A literary bit of costume drama in a green arena
is the play on boards displayed. Unseen a vernal
comic troupe of guisers romp the wooden glade.

In time I settled for a mental sleight geology
of glades in glaze of English green. The geese
leave turds of green, and green dream-bushes in a green
arena. I have well enjoyed myself for nigh on
more nor forty year in gritstone delf, a mile up
out of Mytholmroyd. The world of wooden glade is not
as yet, not undestroyed, but opened to a deeper
sort of void, with sycamore and horse chestnut,
wicken, (that is, rowan, also mountain ash); with
blackbird, nuthatch, flitting tits: a place for me
to read and write and piss. In time I ran a pipe
from running water in the clough to this my old-
discarded turquoise bathroom suite: sink, upturned
pedestal and bath to make a sort of water-feature:
water watering a bog of gunnerah, of ramsons
and of mollyblobs, (that is the kingcup or the marsh
mallow). It offers refuge to a multitude of frog.

Stage-hands may paint the flats of moorland scenery,
but I prefer real flaight of brownery and brief
midsummer greenery, with boggart and with Robin Hood
in local dreamery for an imaginary memory: a mirror-
phase contains the conscience of the self in infant days.

Harold Macmillan blew our brand-new hydrogen bomb up
on an island out at sea somewhere in the Pacific, with
a mushroom cloud predictably terrific. I discovered
an equivalent explosion of my own: up on a rope
slung from our backyard sycamore. I frotted to my
high dry peak and broke into the glade
of heart's content through fine ecstatic pinklesqueaks.

All overhead stood clouds, a spire, and chimneystacks.
I had no thoughts as yet about the other sex.

Aye me, the voice of old experience says that
there's lots of moss up tops, and there we find
some paths back through the past have been foreclosed.
There's a cross at the top of the pass. The ghost
trespasses heather, mosscrop, (that is cottongrass)
and stands as gritstone over aeons of bad weather.

A fine rain coats the earth this morning in
a cold wet fog. This line of thought is sunk
in sphagnum bog. Cheer up! The sun comes clearing.
Scattered clouds are being dogged by scattered breezes.
Scattered hounds around the distance bray.
Scenes that are gone tomorrow have been here today.

Scenes that are gone tomorrow have been here today
as wraith-drifts waft along the path across the pass.
The stoop-stone ghost stands lookout on a wild
and waste wet land. Glum pine stands border
the beyond. One's own regrets cling to the boots
like clay. Body and soul, I like to say are
bedrock grit and porous shale, and flesh as pale bent grass.

I'm six and sunk in thinking in and on upon
the rich deep stench of an Elsan. The sun
beats down on corrugated iron overhead. I wonder
who I am, while other ones play football out
across the sand. The sounds are splash and laughing. But
how come I am who I am, not someone else at all?

And so it was as once upon a bench along
a long green hallway. I had found the key
beneath the donkey-stone, upon the whitewashed
window-sill. I entered my own private wooden glade,
like when I lay in bed with flu in nineteen-fifty-two
just when the King was dead. The glade was then
two minutes long. Some several decades pass by
before the cars are all departing from the crematorium.

The spirits in the Park Wood garden trees appear
subdued. The dead end of the glade is God is dead.
They say he had a son, Adam or someone. That was
long ago and now he's gone. The land is waste.
There's only ghost-speech in the garden. Sycamore
is rotted, and the rope is also gone. There's no more
leaping to the rope from on the dustbin lid,
where I could frot for love of life and physical relief.

In time the escapades of Thingum meet
the escapades of Quim. Thingum is dumb. Quim
takes him by the hand to Quim's bed room
to play like babes themselves in a wooden glade.

In linguistic sludge a slovenly man thinks
slattern, slut and slum. Haslam has come
united and as soon untied: the brief shelf life
of selfish pride. The lass leans on her kitchen sink.
A lad's unrolling tights from her protruding bum.
There's some excitement to the crudely rude. He tries
from here to slip inside. The culmination of this
rum affair takes place up on the landing of
the flight of stairs. Time brings some understanding.

Linguistic sludge invents confessions of the squalid.
It was sweet. She was complaisant, and they both felt
jelly-wobbles. The pun on physical relief is cast
triumphantly, a condom to the bin. There was no sin.
The issues riddle from bare tops to works down bottoms.

Or happen in some innocent winsome bewilderment
Thingum and Quim complicit in some seed discharge
exchange disclosure. Quim takes Thingum by the hand, has
led him to her bed: a pair prepared for mutual exposure.

This verse is like a pinfold for some vulgar word enclosure:
cock, cunt, fuck, suck, such rank bedroom stuff in
say a quiet railway town tucked under Winter Hill.

Psyche and Anthropos were copulating then
like Thingum and the vulvous Quim. This means
fertility like spring is sprung. Thingum is growing
sprouts. Would Psyche like to see the geezer blow?
Psyche would not. Come Thingum hubby just come home.
There's some misunderstanding then. We're back among
the rootlessness of *slang* and *slum*, and slump back in
with bastard orphans, the unfortunates of language.

So much for slutch and such. Such drama-dances
have been played in wooden glades for ages.
Effluent threads of much illusion all unspool
to swim and spoil the shady pool of soul. The snakes
in dressing-gowns are seen beseeching undines for a
what they call a waternymphellation. Art the heart
of privy parts disgraces wastes of space. Lips kiss the face.

Refined is sweet white sugar love, but honey made by bees
in heather, that is stickier and sweeter, but the sweetest
singsong's one of sexual relief. It's soggy in the moss up tops
with leaking sikes and trickles down the ruddy
bracken banks. Tears reach the ears: a lassie lies supine.
A sour-sweet stench of disbelief arises from the sheets.

However sexual, *she* is a pronoun, rather textual than real:
composed of nightie, sibilance and crepuscule, seen
bathing in a pool of dimpled shade. The clouds are moods
and leaves like feathers are a falling down. She vanishes
with slipping cottons in the last of summer's spring. Her
water is both wet and clean, and clear and cold. The year
grows old. The long green strings of algal slime flow by.
As image *she* the soul I own embarrasses, embraces me.

The mournful souls process, the churchbells toll.
The traffic stops along the road. I heard it
on the wireless that the King is dead. And here
and now I wonder who I am and is there room for God
inside my head in bed with flu in nineteen-fifty-two.
A blood-red bus stopped dead on the Blackburn road.

Rough rock dips under the seams of coal. The Daubhill
daub gets baked to Daubhill Brick. The brick to stone
divide can only wobble to the North of River Croal.
The gentle ridge to Astley Bridge had been filled in with
terraces and mills. When coal and mills are done with
we begin to see the Smithills hills. Those hills when smoke
was thick only appeared to us in weeks of wakes.

Here it was that Thingum grew, and sprung from
cotton trunks in the deliriums of spring. Thingum
is wrong to sing the bawdy songs of longing for the Quim
or Jenny Greenteeth who would lure him in to swim
among her folds of frothy scum, and wrap him with
her folds of raw wet liver singing spermovum self-uniting.
thingum bathing in th'irriguous caverns of quim.

The cotton mill has long collapsed. A milliard florets
star the millyard floor: all elderpetals fall. The waters
fill the well. Trees root or rot on remnants of the walls.
She's in the mill-lodge slipping cottons by the waterfall.

She's slipping cottons in the spring while all
the drizzle droplets, being small, drift down the wind
and hardly fall. There's trickle-down from up the moor.
The sun looks feeble through the morning mist. Drizzle
sogs the moss up tops. Trickles drip. The sun looks sore.

Thingum the sun, his bud's to blossom come: quick wit
and lithesome, cock on labia or bottom, breast
or belly button, wanting welcome to however long
protended prong. Thingum is come into a foetid messuage.

The pollywiggles dither mouthing at some algal brim.
Thingum is conscious of how odd it is just to be him;
how odd to be within this quim-and-thingum thing
from first unrolling tights over a bum, like in a dirty song,
a pastoral of carousel carousal: ousels sing collapsing in
a lapse between fell haunches in the slide of love along
a long meltwater vale. She's slipping cottons in the spring.

Genetic morphogenesis must have to mate with
genital geology in mulch of such lubricious squelches
plunging shallow depths of Quim in deliquescence,
garlanding a detumescence fallen into giggles
and some wormy wriggles. Squiggles of bacteria
will fester in the trap beneath the sink. The peaks
will be remembered for emitting liquid squeaks.
Bedrock is marriage bed. Was there not shared
that moment of ejaculation on the landing stairs?
That mouth with its vaginal hairs? Days die and dry
a crust to dust: a wedded pair exist in lack of trust.

She may have been no more than an imaginary pronoun.
I am who I am, a me the same as some small soul
now reaching for the sneck to lift the latch and race
to the back door must pass by lilac tree and brick-red
air-raid shelter and the garage door to reach
and find the key beneath the donkey-stone up on
the whitewashed window-ledge. And then the
black back door will open to the cellar door
with all its coaly depths below, and we can
go down there to know our self and what we've
come here for: to find a meaning in my me being me.

Stone steps lead down into the coal-hole, fed
by chute from the back yard. A wooden staircase
rises overhead. Beside the cellar door there is
a hallway leading to a little-used front door.
There is no cooking in the kitchen done. By now
the range is obsolete. There is a step down to the
scullery. We find a gas-stove and a sink and here
is the contraption for to wash our clothes within.
A door leads to the pantry with a stoneware tub
to keep the eggs in isinglass inside of in. The door
now to our right is to the back of the garage.

Back to the cellar door, and there's a hallway to our right
again. A memory is not at all the same as dream, but rather
as a dream remembered is the dining room in which we do
not dine or not until we get a television set in nineteen-
fifty-seven. It's up and down to me to fetch the coal from
cellar depths and light the fire by which we eat and watch
the black-and-white. Still ticks the tall clock in the hall. The
bench across from the nursery we children tidy up or not.
And our unused front room will hold the telephone.
Eagley One Nine O Two. The house was sold just as I
went to college in the year of nineteen-sixty-five.

The reader of poetic relish happen learns to love
a sinking thinking feeling: sticky squalor of a
rubber johnny dangling from a shrinking head,
drawn off by fingers to a viscous thread.
I mean this as an image of a tristesse tryst, a
sense of we have somehow something missed,
and our bewilderment at absences is
literally lost in mist. The soul says sense of this
cannot be undismissed. The cosmopolitan insists
it's not the size it's what you do with it that
matters like a boil of pus or fisted gist and splatter.
The dumb lad here had wanted to have Thingum kissed.

Some images are spun from bum and sink,
or fingers leading fingers up the stair to form
an image of a mutuality in willing. And he hardly
is aware that his excitement is to do with prospect
of ejaculation, soon or all-too-soon. She had already
fed some sherry to her baby and we must not shout
because her father, home from nightshift snores
through bedroom plasterboard next door.
And next a squelch of come like yeast in fizz aroma
passing orgasmic epiphany complicitly into a coma.

Life is shared with lust and crablice. Pathos treads
the beastly path, squeamish regret for squalors past.
And we could use a sense of sin encompassing
the groans under the stars or stairs and an
intensity's past tense turned unintense and
senseless as the pitch sad being has got stuck in.

Naked poetic numbers in a wooden glade run
dumbly grumbling, crumbling, stumbling on. An
Holy Fool fallen in Folly Hole fetched up in fossil coal.

How slow old industry falls fast into the past!
I've seen the nightshift sweating over cottons down
in Heaven's bottom mill, where angel overlookers
seek with whips a rodent genie in the engine shed.
Just then my earplugs fell into a pool of oil down on
the concrete floor. Pick up and plug the lugs again.

The key up on the windowledge beneath the donkey stone,
the key to the back door and the hallway of green
is key for me to memory, the me I own and all I've seen
and the stupidity, stupendous, of my poetry.
I locked the door behind me back in nineteen-fifty-three.

Me being me as I am all being well would
hope to grow from boy to man who can remember
hallway, mat, settee. And here come my progenitors
come knocking on the locked back door when I
was just about to find the key to me being me.

Me being me the same then as when sometime
later on, a flood had gouged the bank-side tip
and washed off ash and cinder: potsherds gleam
beneath the flow now running clear and long green
algal strings resume their life and glimmer green
as green a green was ever morn or even seen.

Tables were drilled by rote, another word
of unknown root. By heart feels much more cordial.
I had some hope I might resuscitate the art by care
of roots to root a poetry in privy parts and flowering
the written radish of the heart, seeding the gist
of jest, a jewel heart locked in the human chest.
This just is a plea for justice for my lucence lost,
myself obsessed, processed, possessed and re-
possessed by loss. I guess I'll sleep with spoils of coal
put out up on the moor in th'old coal-delvers' hole.

The soul or ghost of cold emission leaves deposits on
the soles of boots sunk twixt the sphagnum and
the peaty soil. All born that shall have lived when they are
dead cannot recall such as the long green hall, the fairground
at Moor Lane: black peas, pink candy floss,
loud garish music, garish light, nor how
the rain makes cinder gravel shine and stains the mind.
Can it remain beyond, behind, a dying brain?

By gate, by windowledge, by key in the door, but why
I locked it when I'd come inside? A long settee
along a long green hallway and a great grand-
father clock. Now who am I and how come I
am me and are they knocking on the locked back door?

I have seen Memory a-humping Dream. That's how
my story was conceived. Me and she, then, we were
stuck among the rocks and bushes of a muddy carr
before a pair of tractor-tyres come backing down
the bank to hook and pull us off the soggy moss,
a favour without charge. But who were we?
Was she some succubus to suck and drain us off
to dregs and dross? We lie exhausted for our loss.

Thought spent a long ejaculation on vacation in the *slums*,
a little orphan of our etymology. And was it my
selfconsciousness invented *soul*? O Soul Thou
Sleeping Fruit and Beauty! *Cute* is an aphetic of
acute. O Radiance of Spirit! I see thee thou
enshawled, O Soul Thou Waterfall! The sprawl
of thee my soul is all my eye. Now I can see the me
has been too shy at times to do his reproductive duty.

Light fails, a flour of snow falls over stony ears.
I think it's dusk and now I can't make out my written
squiggles, wriggles. There are giggles in my signatural style,
however squatted in the garden wild, of wooden glade,
a disused delf or else, an elf, the child myself.

In Dormer House on Dormer Street in Astley Bridge in
Bolton: Titumtitum Titumtitum Titumtitum *et cetera:*
The nursery at the back of the house was next to the front
door. And Dormer Street were nought but cobbled ginnel.
It was on Newnham Street my grandma called me off
from playing cricket with the streetlads and the lamp-post
for a wicket. From there the great black backyard gate
stood out beside a cinder snicket, our big house my boast.

There was a youth as found a lass to love
on Gaskell Street, that's now demolished. She would
feed her rats on Mother's Pride. Thieves had already
stripped the lead from out the privy shed. A mattress
on the cold flag ground was all she had for bed.
Damp rises by a process of osmosis. There's a smell.
He was a scholar to appreciate the atmosphere of squalor.
That was just as well. And in her parlour by the fire
that lass was right well generous with coal.

Some ecstasies less fleshly were for me more
immaterial. I saw a lass once brush her hair, her hand held
high her hair-dryer. There was a scattering like stars
in air, of an electrical elastic static, and it spits and flits
with little spirits wick and fair. I caught some for
an image for the brain-store of a life ecstatic.

Middle classes may pay for the better classes: Latin
grammar and the English classics. I was shifted to a school
with a real gymnasium, and soon I had my little pinkle
rubbing up against the rope to come to my high dry
ecstatic tinkles through the brain: orgastic rapture-capture.
So I got my dad to fix a rope to our sycamore tree.

So I was taught by tautened rope and Pocket
Oxford Dictionary: masturbation means my
self-abuse. Toss off and wank were like tabooed.
Slang is another bastard of the language, and
matriculation is another game. The masters
pointed me towards the colleges with spires and there
the fellows can't excuse my poorly French and so
to France I have to go for there they speak that tongue.
And so on Saint John's Eve I climbed in company
the Puy-de-Dome. The road went round in bends.
A lad had offered me a fag and lit it up for me
and lights spread out across the valley all the way to Vichy.
O Tobacco thou shall be my friend for life and happen
be the death of me now smoking roll-ups at computer
or upon my bed! I can't regret the years on cigarettes.
They've had a power to modulate a life's epiphanous pips.

Here's an epiphanous pip one winter just popped up:
A robin sips at an icicle tip, and stutters subsong
soft and low to nothing in particular but glitter,
frost and snow. Then of a sudden hear him blow!
Or when the King was dead and me in bed with flu.
That was in nineteen-fifty-two. Alive and not yet dead.

For two minutes' eternity a blood-red bus was stood
on the Blackburn road, and there I fell into infinity.
The King is dead. I'm nearly five and ill but yet alive.

One day the soul invented the illusion of a psychic depth
of pure imagination, the reflection of the deeps
of shallow light. One day the soul set sail across
an ocean of geography and history, of metaphor,
of watery mystery. Soul strokes the implement it has to
calibrate transcendent grounded oracles for home,
a county country where the waters are all drawn across
a mossy plain. A spooked Lancastrian grins comic pain.

The soul, now bored has but to index, to alphabetise
the front to back and gate and latch; the reach for arms
upon a tree; the wooden glade and shield my grandpa
round at Holly Bank had made for me, all for to fight
the frightful cock that ruled the sizable back yard;
the lilac and the air-raid shelter and the shade of war;
the wank; the coal and soot and smoke; the key;
the cottons and the green settee; and whether God
exists or not, as I do. I am me. And now I hear them
knocking and complaining at the locked back door

I saw my father give that bird the chop one Sunday
Morning on the block. The churchbells rang. The boys'
brigade tuned up to march to church down Newnham Street
from the Parochial Hall. They had their banner to unfurl.
I saw the cock's head drop, the body run and drop. Fresh
drops now gloss the yard as glade in daze. Drops stop.

Re-do, go through settee and flu in nineteen-fifty-two,
a bus stood still on Blackburn Road; the glaze of wooden
glade; the sullen sun on hazy days; the ways of daze;
the crazy blues and fancy dances and ejaculate mischances;
litter left in the abandoned works. The sycamore
heart-rotted; rope, dustbin lid and thrill all gone.

The fay or fey or furry fairies of a moor I've courted
or pretended to for more nor forty year and ramble-
ambled in the brambled woods of Sowerby Ramble.
Mills are all or mostly fallen. More moors up over yon.

This sense and sentiment of love for odd lost lasses, what's
all that about? A schoolboy on a storage heater told me:
think your dirty thought, it grows, you tap it. Another lad
said wrap it in a scrap of paper, frenzy, go, go, go.

Infertile are the great plateaux enclosing wooden glades
of bliss, composing blues most lachrymose and those
twice-weekly treats. There came an age of flannel passage,
short to long, and mother now inspects bedsheets.
In all conscience, can tossing-off be wrong?

Young bullock wankers chew the grass and bide the time
when they'll be lured by heifer lasses one by one.
The lasses try to tire them out. I've wondered what
the heck that's all about. The courting kye kiss
as they pass the col of coloured masses. Mating collars
them and I in them: my path from high and dry through
springs of sticky wet, peaks on a rope to peaks together
with her in the heather in the weather clouding
Wood Head Grove, a glade, the woodness of Wood Royd,
glad sharing yards and yards of squeaks and groans;
the boggart springing in a nest of naked furry fairies.

One spell of a wooden glade is a material, a splinter
in the finger in a wood-shed's shade, but some are
immaterially made, summer or winter. Something broke
upon the edge of night: eggyolk spilled over beds of cloud,
soundlessly loud up on that summit with a crowd.

Sing Wilson Johnson Charles de Gaulle: all fallen
down through deep time's hole. I stood up in
some company up on the Dome. A bed of cloud
spread round, flouncing with misty fluff and stuff,
sky blue, the lemon sole, and sun's egg yolk:
For joy I threw my hat into the cloud and headed home.

That was a Robin Hood, a feathered trilby and
the builders up on scaffolding sang (Macmillan
Kennedy De Gaulle again) *Where* did you *get* that hat,
where did you get *that hat*? From a market stall in the
market hall and it cost all of fourteen-shillings-and-six-
pence. Half a day's wage! A lad with more money than
sense! I sacrificed it to the clouds. And that was that.

That crowd disperses as the clouding rises and I head
back down in cloud and hazy glades of wooden void.
I have seen such a dawn and want to write it down.
I come down as a kind of clown passed through the cloud
into a land, leven or laund or lawn. The morn
of mist was misty morn strung through like lyric lyres
in scrubby underwood. I do enjoy the feeling being lyrical,
forlorn, but undestroyed, sublimely happy I was born

to live at Foster Clough a mile up out of Mytholmroyd.

Lightning Source UK Ltd.
Milton Keynes UK
UKHW010732100320
360091UK00001B/73